TO:

_____

FROM:

_____

DATE:

_____

# JOURNAL

# THROUGH

# THE

# *Bible*

## EXPLORE
*Genesis to Revelation*

Thomas Nelson

**THOMAS NELSON**
Since 1798

*Printed in India*

20 21 22 23 24  BRI  5 4 3 2 1

# *Introduction*

elcome to *Journal Through the Bible*! You're about to start a life-changing journey through God's Word—a year of living, exploring, and absorbing the truths He has revealed to us. Each day, as you settle into a comfortable spot with your journal and your Bible, you're going to have your eyes opened to a new part of God's eternal story—and your story.

So as you begin, as in any journey, it helps to set your direction and gather what you'll need. Practically, you're in good shape; start with this guide, a notebook, a study Bible, and access to a variety of trusted commentaries, dictionaries, and online resources. Perhaps have in mind a few people you could talk with about what comes up during your reading and journaling. At the beginning of each session, bring your sense of curiosity and a commitment to honesty. Bring an open heart and open mind. And, of course, pray. Pray for the guidance of the Holy Spirit, to know God better, and for the wisdom to learn more about how and where God is leading you.

It's important to leave a few things behind too—like stress. Don't feel like you have to have an epiphany every single time you read and reflect. No need to twist yourself into some sort of spiritual pretzel, trying to have all the "right" responses. Don't worry about sticking to a particular schedule either. If you're not feeling particularly plugged in spiritually right now, or if you feel stuck, it's okay to take a pause. Just keep returning to the Word, inviting it and its Author into your life again and again, day by day. God tells us that He will honor those who diligently seek Him (Hebrews 11:6). As you seek Him in the pages of your Bible and in your journal this year, you will find Him, and yourself, in astounding new ways.

# Old Testament

# Genesis

In the beginning God created the heavens and the earth.

GENESIS 1:1

· · · · · · · · · · · · · · · · · · · · · · · · · · · · · ·

## READING PLAN
17 days; 3 chapters a day

## THEMES
origins of mankind; entrance of sin; beginnings of civilization;
God's chosen people

## MAJOR PLAYERS
Abraham and Sarah, Adam and Eve, Cain and Abel, Esau,
Isaac and Rebekah, Ishmael and Hagar, Jacob, Leah, Rachel,
Joseph, Lot, Melchizedek, Methuselah, Noah, the serpent,
Seth, Shem, Ham, Japheth

· · · · · · · · · · · · · · · · · · · · · · · · · · · · · ·

## Background

Genesis is humankind's origin story and the foundation of the
entire Bible. It's part of the Pentateuch, or first five books of the
Bible, a.k.a. the "Torah" or "Law." These books are also known as
the books of Moses, which he assembled to instruct the Israelites
on their way to the Promised Land. The book of Genesis covers
the story of God and His people from "the beginning" of time to
circa 1800 BC, approximately three hundred years before Moses.
Take your time with this book because it will be key to understanding the rest of your journey through the Bible.

# Summary

In Genesis we begin at the beginning—of human history and of the great, sweeping story of God and the humans He created. Chapters 1–11 discuss / detail / describe human history in general, and chapters 12–50 concentrate on the family of Abraham and his descendants, or the "patriarchs." In chapters 1–11, you'll read the beautiful creation hymn, passed down for generations until it reached Moses. You'll meet Adam and Eve, see the entrance of sin into the world, and witness the first murder in the story of Cain and Abel. You'll read about Noah and the flood, his sons, and the nations that grew from them. Finally, the Tower of Babel tells of the division of mankind along language lines.

The second part of Genesis, 12–50, begins with Abraham, the "father" of the Hebrew nation. Through his covenant with God, his descendants would outnumber the stars, and all people would be blessed in the eventual coming of Jesus. His son with Hagar, Ishmael, would begin another nation, while his son with Sarah, Isaac, would begin the line of the Hebrews. Isaac and his wife, Rebekah, gave birth to Jacob, who stole his father's blessing and had twelve children who would become the twelve tribes of Israel. Jacob and Rachel's son Joseph, famously sold by his brothers into slavery, would miraculously become a leader of Egypt and save his family from famine. The book ends with the deaths of Jacob and Joseph, but of course, it's just the beginning of the story. Through this line of imperfect people, God would bring about a plan of redemption for all of humanity.

# Reflections

1. As you read and take notes on each section of Genesis, ask yourself a few general questions:

   What does this reveal about God? His personality? His purposes?

   _____

   _____

   _____

   What does this reveal about us? About humankind?

   _____

   _____

   _____

   What does this reveal about the world we live in?

   _____

   _____

   _____

2. Write down the many covenants and promises between God and His people in this book (like the ones between God and His creation, and with Adam, Noah, and Abraham). What do they tell us about God's desires for His people?

   _____

   _____

   _____

3. Consider keeping a family tree of the generations covered in Genesis, paying special attention to the tribe of Judah, out of which Jesus would eventually come. What kind of people are in Jesus' family tree?

_____

_____

_____

_____

4. For fun, look for all the ways someone tricks someone else in Genesis and the way the founders of humankind are always pulling fast ones on one another. How does God work with and through these events despite these constant shenanigans?

_____

_____

_____

_____

5. What does it mean to you that, like this motley cast of characters, you are part of God's story of humankind on earth? How might He be using you as you are now and as you are becoming?

_____

_____

_____

_____

# Exodus

You in Your mercy have led forth the people whom
You have redeemed; You have guided them in
Your strength to Your holy habitation.

EXODUS 15:13

. . . . . . . . . . . . . . . . . . . . . . . . . . . . . . . . . . . . .

**READING PLAN**
13 days; 3 chapters a day

**THEMES**
redemption; covenant; provision; the founding of Israel

**MAJOR PLAYERS**
Aaron, Jethro, Miriam, Moses, the pharaoh, Zipporah

. . . . . . . . . . . . . . . . . . . . . . . . . . . . . . .

## Background

This second book of Moses picks up approximately three hundred
years after Genesis left off at the death of Joseph. The Hebrews
became enslaved in Egypt after a regime change, and they cried
out to be freed. *Exodus* means "exit" or "departure." The exit of
the Hebrews from Egypt is debated as having occurred on one
of these two dates: circa 1440 BC or 1290 BC. Depending on
the year, the pharaoh might have been Amenhotep II (1453 BC)
or Ramses II (1304 BC).

# Summary

In the first half of Exodus, you'll read the action-packed story of Moses and the Israelites' escape from Egypt. In the second half, you'll see instructions for the tabernacle (God's holy dwelling) and the priesthood. The book begins with Moses' origin story, his forty years as an adopted son in the Egyptian royal family and his forty years as a fugitive in the desert. At age eighty, he encountered God in the form of a burning bush and received a mission to free God's people. Reluctantly, with the help of his brother, Aaron, he confronted the pharaoh, demanding that he let God's people go. The pharaoh's refusal resulted in ten grisly plagues; in the final plague, the angel of death "passed over" Hebrew homes that had been painted in the blood of pure lambs.

You'll read about the Hebrews' dramatic exit from Egypt and escape through the Red Sea. While they set out through the wilderness, God provided guidance through a pillar of cloud and fire; food through manna and quail; and water from a rock. Then, critically, He gave Moses the Ten Commandments, the foundation of Hebrew Law and our standard for holy attitudes toward God and other people. In the story of the golden calf, you'll see the first of many cycles of God's people toward idolatry and back to God again. God then gave Moses instructions for His holy tabernacle, a place of worship and a reminder of His presence in the middle of the people's camp. All of its symbolic aspects were there to remind them of His covenant, His provision, and His guidance.

# Reflections

1. Based on Moses' choices and actions, how would you describe him? What does it mean to you that God chose to rescue His nation through Moses?

_____

_____

_____

_____

_____

_____

_____

_____

2. How does this book show that God equips the called, instead of calling the equipped? How does this make you feel about your own calling? Do you trust that God equips you just as He equipped Moses and Aaron?

_____

_____

_____

_____

_____

_____

_____

_____

3. What parts of the Exodus story tell us most about how God feels about His people? How He listens to them? How He speaks to them? What He is prepared to do for them?

_____

_____

_____

_____

_____

_____

_____

_____

_____

4. What do God's commandments, the ark of the covenant, and the instructions for the tabernacle tell us about Him? How do these things prioritize reverence? How can we prioritize reverence today in our laid-back world?

_____

_____

_____

_____

_____

_____

_____

_____

# Leviticus

"I am the LORD who brings you up out of the land of Egypt,
to be your God. You shall therefore be holy, for I am holy."

LEVITICUS 11:45

. . . . . . . . . . . . . . . . . . . . . . . . . . . . . .

## READING PLAN
10 days; 2.5 chapters a day

## THEMES
laws; rituals; regulations for the holiness of God's people

## MAJOR PLAYERS
Israelite people, Levites (Israel's priests and priestly assistants),
Moses

. . . . . . . . . . . . . . . . . . . . . . . . . . . . . .

## Background

As part of the Pentateuch, or first five books of the Bible, scholars
traditionally attribute authorship to Moses, who passed on God's
laws to the people at Sinai. Dated from 1450 to 1410 BC, Moses
wrote this book as a handbook for the Levites, God's priests.

## Summary

The Levites were one of the twelve tribes of Israel, descended
from Levi. They were priests for all of Israel, as well as assistants,
judges, teachers, and personnel for the tabernacle and temple.
They were supported by tithes from the other eleven tribes, and

they had varied and detailed responsibilities. This book is a manual for their work with sacrifices, offerings, and rules for daily living and governance. When you read, you may find some of these statutes odd, shocking, severe, or even funny (please, only eat bugs with jointed legs, and lay off the geckos). However they may seem to us now, they reflect a God who is interested in every corner of His people's daily lives and who would protect them from anything that could undermine or weaken them as a civilization. Pay special attention to the sacrifices described in Leviticus; they'll come back up again in relation to Jesus' sacrifice for us.

## Reflections

1. As you read, keep track of the different kinds of sacrifices and offerings and why the people made them. Knowing Christ acts as our final sacrifice, are there any reasons in your life that signal you to turn to Him?

 

 

 

 

2. Do you believe God still wants to be involved in every corner of your life? What areas in your life can you ask Him in to, even though they may seem mundane?

 

 

 

 

 

3. Do tradition and ritual play any part in your faith practice? If so, look into the meanings behind the traditions you practice, and examine any relation they might have to Jesus' atonement for your sins. How do traditions and rituals make you feel connected to God's people who practiced the Levitical rituals and laws?

_____

_____

_____

_____

_____

4. God set aside special days for feasts of remembrance, worship, repentance, rest, and renewal. How might celebrating feast days for the same reasons deepen your faith?

_____

_____

_____

_____

_____

5. Were you ever made to follow rules that you didn't understand, but they turned out to benefit you in some way? Which rules in Leviticus stand out to you as a reflection of a Father's love for His set-apart people?

_____

_____

_____

_____

_____

# Numbers

"Take a census of all the congregation of the children of
Israel. . . . You and Aaron shall number them by their armies."

NUMBERS 1:2–3

. . . . . . . . . . . . . . . . . . . . . . . . . . . . . . . . . .

## READING PLAN
16 days; 2.25 chapters a day

## THEMES
Israel's forty years of wandering; organization of the people;
challenges and grace on the way to the Promised Land

## MAJOR PLAYERS
Aaron, Balaam, Balak, Caleb, Joshua, Korah, Miriam, Moses

. . . . . . . . . . . . . . . . . . . . . . . . . . . . . . . .

## Background

At the beginning of Moses' fourth book, the people had been
encamped at Mount Sinai for approximately two years. Numbers
starts with a census, or numbering (hence the name of the book),
and continues through the next thirty-eight years of wandering
in the desert.

# Summary

After Moses had received the Law, it was time to organize and move the people toward the Promised Land. The census at the opening of Numbers counted only the men of fighting age, but scholars estimate that the Israelites numbered approximately two million in total. Moses and Aaron organized the men into armies, regulated the camps and marching orders, made offerings, and set out. Along the way, you'll see how Moses faced mess after mess, from complaining and griping people, to challenges to his authority, to plagues, fires, and attacking locals. Still, the cloud of the Lord instructed them on when to stay and go, and Moses pleaded for God's mercy on the people again and again.

So why did they wander so long over such a short distance? At one point, they were on the edge of the Promised Land, and Moses sent out twelve spies to assess the situation. They reported that the land was a beautiful and fertile place but filled with frightening enemies. Only two spies, Caleb and Joshua, wanted to go forward. The rest wanted to turn back. At the edge of their promise, they faltered—and God made it so that none of them, except Caleb and Joshua, would enter the land. Due to his disobedience, Moses would only view it from a mountaintop.

Numbers covers not only numerical data and regulations of life in the camp but also the cycle of unbelief met with consequences, and then Moses' intercession, and then God's mercy.

# Reflections

1. Note the times and reasons Moses and Aaron have to intercede and pray that God will save the people from the consequences of their actions. What does it mean to you that Jesus does the interceding for us today?

_____

_____

_____

_____

_____

_____

_____

2. Think about the possibility that God may have let the people wander not only as punishment but also as a way to teach them, preserve them from harm, and let the surrounding nations know that these were His people. How do you see this happening in Numbers?

_____

_____

_____

_____

_____

_____

_____

_____

3. Can you think of a time when this happened in your life? A time of "wandering" that taught you, preserved you, or made you a witness to others? How did God meet you in that time?

_____

_____

_____

_____

_____

_____

_____

_____

_____

4. What were the results of the people's lack of trust in God? Of Moses' lack of trust? When you are short on trust, how do you deal with it? What helps you return to God?

_____

_____

_____

_____

_____

_____

_____

_____

_____

_____

# Deuteronomy

Hear, O Israel: The LORD our God, the LORD is one!
You shall love the LORD your God with all your heart,
with all your soul, and with all your strength.

DEUTERONOMY 6:4–5

. . . . . . . . . . . . . . . . . . . . . . . . . . . . .

READING PLAN
12 days; 2.75 chapters a day

THEMES
restatement of the most important laws for the new generation;
preparing to enter the Promised Land

MAJOR PLAYERS
Joshua, Moses

. . . . . . . . . . . . . . . . . . . . . . . . . . . . .

## Background

The final book of Moses is his farewell to the people. The next generation had risen up and was ready to enter Canaan, the Promised Land. It is dated circa 1406 BC, with the last chapter's authorship attributed most often to Joshua.

# Summary

Moses knew the end of his life was approaching, and within view of the Promised Land, he summarized the most important points, laws, and lessons of the Israelites' wandering in the wilderness. *Deuteronomy* means "second law" or "repetition of the law," but it is more than just a rehashing. Verses from this book are quoted often in the New Testament, most notably by Jesus as He responded to Satan during His temptation. Deuteronomy is the basis of the prophets' message in the rest of the Old Testament. And this book is, for us, a way to learn from the history, laws, and even the mistakes of God's people. Moses took the new generation through a retrospective of their spiritual history, emphasizing how important it was to study, honor, and teach God's Word.

Deuteronomy is set up as a treaty between God and the people, including the consequences of breaking the Law and the benefits of keeping it. Moses used this opportunity to recap daily laws on subjects small and large, showing how much God cared about justice in every aspect of their lives. He reminded them of feasts to be celebrated in remembrance of God's goodness and for social unity. Moses emphasized that their covenant with God would bring them life and that all other ways would bring death. He left them with a song and blessing, and then Moses went atop Mount Nebo to view the Promised Land, where he died. Joshua, Moses' successor, was left with the task of moving the people into the Promised Land.

# Reflections

1. What are the most oft-repeated, reinforced points Moses wanted to leave with the Israelites? How are these points still relevant today?

_____

_____

_____

_____

_____

_____

_____

2. Consider how important it is to review history, learn from it, and not repeat the mistakes of our ancestors. What can we learn from Moses' generation? What about generations in our time?

_____

_____

_____

_____

_____

_____

_____

_____

3. How does Moses emphasize the importance of God's Word? As you journal through the Bible, how has reading and learning more about God's Word affected your life so far?

_____

_____

_____

_____

_____

_____

_____

_____

4. While some of these laws and regulations were specific to the people during their time, many are still easily applicable to us today. What do these laws tell us about God's attitude toward His people, His character, and His goals for them? For us today?

_____

_____

_____

_____

_____

_____

_____

_____

_____

# Joshua

"Be strong and of good courage, for to this people you shall divide as an inheritance the land which I swore to their fathers to give them."

JOSHUA 1:6

. . . . . . . . . . . . . . . . . . . . . . . . . . . . . .

## READING PLAN
7 days; 3.5 chapters a day

## THEMES
taking hold of the Promised Land; faith and obedience; courage

## MAJOR PLAYERS
Joshua, Rahab, tribes of Israel

. . . . . . . . . . . . . . . . . . . . . . . . . . . . . .

## Background

Joshua is the first of the Historical Books of the Bible, a bridge between Moses' books and the nation of Israel's entry into the Promised Land. While the book's author is anonymous, tradition says Joshua started it and a high priest completed it. It is dated to the mid-1400s BC; be sure to check out the fascinating archeological discoveries surrounding the cities mentioned in this book.

## Summary

Moses had died within view of the Promised Land, and leadership fell to his assistant, Joshua. God was with him and told him many times to have courage as he led the people into Canaan. The first half of the book covers the conquest of the Promised Land, starting with Jericho and Israel's miraculous, wall-tumbling victory there. God continued to show up for Israel in incredible ways as they campaigned across the region, though they were still prone to faithlessness and errors of judgment. Nonetheless, God brought them into the land. The second half of the book covers land division between Israel's tribes and their restoration after forty years of wandering.

## Reflections

1. Write down how many times God told Joshua and His people to "be courageous." What situations were they in? How did they respond? How did God provide? In what areas could God be calling you to be courageous?

_____

_____

_____

_____

2. God had promised Canaan to Israel, so it was basically theirs already. All they had to do was trust Him and lay hold of the blessings of Canaan sitting in front of them. Are there any promises of God that you have yet to lay hold of? If so, what is stopping you?

_____

_____

_____

_____

_____

3. Joshua warned the people about idolatry, a recurring problem for them. They were in danger of taking on the gods of their neighbors. But Joshua declared, "As for me and my house, we will serve the LORD" (24:15). If you make this declaration for yourself, what kinds of things in today's culture will you choose *not* to serve?

_____

_____

_____

_____

_____

_____

_____

4. At the end of the book, Joshua set up a stone memorial or altar to celebrate God keeping His covenant. What kinds of battles has God helped you through? How can you set up metaphorical "altars or memorials" to remind you of how God has helped you through your battles and of His goodness?

_____

_____

_____

_____

_____

_____

_____

# Judges

In those days there was no king in Israel; everyone
did what was right in his own eyes.

JUDGES 21:25

. . . . . . . . . . . . . . . . . . . . . . . . . . . . . . . .

## READING PLAN
8 days; 2.5 chapters a day

## THEMES
cycle of sin; consequences and deliverance; God using the weak
to fulfill His purposes

## MAJOR PLAYERS
Abimelech, Amalekites, Ammonites, Arabians, Barak,
Deborah, Delilah, Gideon, Jael, Jephthah, Midianites,
Moabites, Philistines, Samson, Sisera

. . . . . . . . . . . . . . . . . . . . . . . . . . . . . . . .

## Background

Judges takes place after Joshua died and covers nonchronological
events during a period of 300–400 years, circa 1400–1100 BC.
The author is anonymous, but tradition points to Samuel, writing
circa 1050–1000 BC.

# Summary

After Joshua's generation died out, the Israelites fell into disunity and idolatry, picking up their neighbors' habits as well as their false gods. At that time their government was a *theocracy,* led directly by God. But they launched into a cycle of forgetting God, being oppressed by other people, crying out to God, and being rescued. In response to their cries, God raised up judges not only to govern the people but also to lead battles against those who would destroy them. Here we see a civilization continually approaching the brink of destruction and being miraculously saved by God every time. You'll read some grim and grisly tales in this book, but you'll also see a God who continually steps in to save His people.

# Reflections

1. As you read, write down some of the odd things Israelites used for weapons (millstone, tent peg, jawbone of a donkey, etc.). This seems to complement God using odd items (and ill-suited people) to win a victory—or using the weak to put the mighty to shame (1 Corinthians 1:27). How has God used something odd or ill-suited in your life to bring victory?

---

---

---

---

---

2. In Judges, as the people descend into separation from God, we hear the same refrain: "Everyone did what was right in [their] own eyes" (Judges 21:25). How did this lead to disaster for them? How does it for us? Have you ever followed your own desires and found yourself lost?

_____

_____

_____

_____

_____

3. With each judge, the people went through a predictable cycle (rebellion, consequences, repentance, salvation). Have you personally seen this cycle in action? How does it comfort you to know that God offers restoration?

_____

_____

_____

_____

_____

4. How would you describe Gideon's leadership? Have you ever suffered from "impostor syndrome" like him? How did God encourage him, and how does that encourage you in the things you're called to?

_____

_____

_____

_____

# Ruth

Ruth said: "Entreat me not to leave you, or to turn back from following
after you; for wherever you go, I will go; and wherever you lodge,
I will lodge; your people shall be my people, and your God, my God."

\textsc{Ruth 1:16}

. . . . . . . . . . . . . . . . . . . . . . . . . . . . . . .

## READING PLAN
1 day; 4 chapters a day

## THEMES
loyalty; redemption; dedication; family acceptance

## MAJOR PLAYERS
Boaz, Naomi, Orpah, Ruth

. . . . . . . . . . . . . . . . . . . . . . . . . . . . . . .

## Background

Jewish tradition tells us that Samuel wrote this book, though the
book is anonymous. The author wrote it to show the lineage of
a newly anointed King David, likely circa 1011–970 BC. It's set
during the time of the judges.

## Summary

This is a story of love and loyalty—and of how God redeems.
Ruth wasn't born a Jew, but she made Naomi's God her God.
Boaz was a descendant of Rahab, another Gentile woman.

Still, God made them direct ancestors of Christ. Today Boaz is considered a "type" of Jesus, and Ruth, the bride of Christ or the church. That's because Boaz, a distant relative of Naomi, acted as a kinsman-redeemer—a relative who marries a widow and takes her under his protection. As you read Ruth's story, you'll see a beautiful picture of how Christ welcomes us into His family.

## Reflections

1. Which of Ruth's qualities impressed Boaz and Naomi? Which ones impress you? How can you make those qualities a bigger part of your life and faith?

_____

_____

_____

_____

_____

2. Family lineage was extremely important to the original readers of this book. What does it say about God that Ruth and Rahab were foreigners, yet He made them ancestors of Jesus?

_____

_____

_____

_____

_____

3. Look back on Rahab's story (Joshua 2). In what ways did she and Ruth take risks to be part of God's family? How were they brave? What is your approach to risk when it comes to following God?

_____

_____

_____

_____

_____

_____

_____

_____

_____

4. What parallels can you find between Boaz as a kinsman-redeemer and Jesus as your Redeemer?

_____

_____

_____

_____

_____

_____

_____

_____

_____

# 1 Samuel

"The Lord does not *see* as man sees; for man looks at the outward appearance, but the Lord looks at the heart."

1 Samuel 16:7

. . . . . . . . . . . . . . . . . . . . . . . . . . . . . .

## READING PLAN
9 days; 3.5 chapters a day

## THEMES
end of the time of the judges; beginning of the monarchy

## MAJOR PLAYERS
Abigail, David, Eli, Goliath, Hannah, Jonathan, Samuel, Saul

. . . . . . . . . . . . . . . . . . . . . . . . . . . . . .

## Background

The author of both books of Samuel is anonymous and could not have been Samuel himself since the text covers his death. First and Second Samuel were originally one book, outlining the end of the time of the judges and the rise of the monarchy in Israel. First Samuel is difficult to date but may be circa 1000 BC.

## Summary

The book of 1 Samuel starts with Samuel's origin story. God called Samuel while he was as a child while under the mentorship of the priest Eli. Samuel became the last judge in the time of the judges; the system had failed, and leadership was corrupt in the priesthood. Samuel was also a priest and a prophet—and he anointed Israel's first and second kings. Samuel was a bridge between these two eras.

The people wanted a king, and though God warned them against it, He let them have their way. Samuel anointed Saul, who initially proved himself worthy. But then Saul's leadership stumbled. He made a spiral of bad decisions because he leaned on his own wisdom instead of God's. So God had to replace King Saul with a man after His own heart. Secretly, God sent Samuel to anoint the shepherd boy David. For years, while Saul continued his disastrous reign, David trained and received the skills he would need. He worked in the palace, defeated the giant Goliath, and became a hero to the people. Jealous, Saul pursued David for years and threatened him with death, but David refused to fight back and kill God's anointed. Eventually Saul fell on his sword in battle, opening the way for a new king.

## *Reflections*

1. What's the difference between what God saw in Saul's heart and what He saw in David's? How can you be more "after" God's heart?

_____

_____

_____

_____

_____

_____

_____

2. What skills and strengths did David gain in his series of less glamorous roles between being anointed and Saul's death? How has God grown you in an in-between time, or how is He growing you now during a difficult time?

_____

_____

_____

_____

_____

3. What can we learn about true friendship from David and Jonathan? How can we become more encouraging to the friends God has placed in our lives?

_____

_____

_____

_____

_____

4. How did Hannah and Abigail display bravery and humility? How have you found this unlikely combination of attributes to be intertwined in Scripture and in your life?

_____

_____

_____

_____

_____

# 2 Samuel

"Your house and your kingdom shall be established forever
before you. Your throne shall be established forever."

2 SAMUEL 7:16

. . . . . . . . . . . . . . . . . . . . . . . . . . . . . . . . . . .

## READING PLAN
7 days; 3.5 chapters a day

## THEMES
David's rule; God's use of imperfect people

## MAJOR PLAYERS
Abner, Absalom, Bathsheba, David, Ishbosheth,
Mephibosheth, Nathan, Uriah

. . . . . . . . . . . . . . . . . . . . . . . . . . . . . . . . . .

## Background

This book covers the reign of King David and dates circa 1010–
970 BC. Second Samuel picks up directly where 1 Samuel ends.

## Summary

Second Samuel tells the story of David's forty-year reign, as
well as the covenant God made with him to establish an eternal
throne through his line—which was fulfilled in Jesus. After Saul
and Jonathan were killed, David mourned. He went to Hebron
in Judah, where he was anointed king, but Saul's house installed

their own heir; the people did not anoint David as the king of all Israel for another seven years. In this book you'll read of David's victories and failures, especially in the case of Bathsheba. The fallout caused years of family violence and tragedy. But David's faith outweighed his faults, and God always sustained David.

# Reflections

1. What was David's approach to the people in Saul's family and to those who tried to benefit from their deaths? What does this tell us about David's priorities?

_____

_____

_____

_____

_____

2. Consider David's actions when the ark was brought to Jerusalem. Do you believe that our worship and joy in turn delights God? How can you be less self-conscious in your worship and thanksgiving?

_____

_____

_____

_____

_____

3. See if you can trace the trail of strife that flowed from David's choices with Bathsheba. How do you deal with harsh consequences of your actions combined with God's presence in your life? How did David?

_____

_____

_____

_____

_____

_____

_____

_____

4. David wrote a thanksgiving psalm and referred to the coming ruler—the Messiah. Try writing your own psalm of thanksgiving, reminding yourself of what God has done in the ups and downs in your life.

_____

_____

_____

_____

_____

_____

_____

_____

# 1 Kings

LORD God of Israel, there is no God in heaven above or on
earth below like You, who keep Your covenant and mercy with
Your servants who walk before You with all their hearts.

1 KINGS 8:23

. . . . . . . . . . . . . . . . . . . . . . . . . . . . . .

## READING PLAN
9 days; 2.5 chapters a day

## THEMES
Solomon's reign and the golden age of Israel; decline of the
nation; Elijah's prophetic ministry

## MAJOR PLAYERS
Elijah, Nathan, Solomon, kings of Israel: Ahab, Ahaziah,
Baasha, Elah, Hoshea, Jehoahaz, Jehu, Jeroboam, Jeroboam
II, Joash, Joram, Menahem, Nadab, Omri, Pekah, Pekahiah,
Shallum, Zechariah, Zimri, kings of Judah: Abijah, Ahaz,
Ahaziah, Amaziah, Amon, Asa, Athaliah (queen), Hezekiah,
Jehoahaz, Jehoiachin, Jehoiakim, Jehoram, Jehoshaphat, Joash,
Josiah, Jotham, Manasseh, Rehoboam, Uzziah, Zedekiah

. . . . . . . . . . . . . . . . . . . . . . . . . . . . . .

## Background

In the Jewish texts, 1 and 2 Kings are combined into one book;
they were divided during translation into Greek. No one knows
the author of these works, but it must have been someone with
access to royal records and historical documents—possibly

Jeremiah, Ezra, or Ezekiel. Whoever it was, he compiled a record of the Hebrew nation that starts with Solomon and continues until the end of David's earthly kingdom, a period of approximately four hundred years. First and Second Kings correspond with the book of 2 Chronicles.

## Summary

In 1 Kings, you'll read about the rise and reign of Solomon, who built God's temple in Jerusalem and presided over a golden age for Israel. While David was a warrior, his son Solomon was a builder and statesman. Solomon's big mistake was marrying hundreds of women, especially from other nations, to build his alliances. After his death, the kingdom divided; ten tribes established a nation to the north (Israel), and the tribes of Judah and Benjamin took the south (Judah). First Kings covers the first eighty years of those kingdoms and their many and various rulers. God sent the fiery prophet Elijah to root out idolatry and call the straying people back to God.

## Reflections

1. Review young Solomon's prayer for wisdom and God's response. How can you prioritize the search for wisdom in your life today?

_____

_____

_____

_____

_____

2. As you get to know the prophet Elijah, think about his actions and characteristics. What did God call him to, and how were his actions tailored to his audience?

_____

_____

_____

_____

_____

3. Start keeping track of all the rulers of Israel and Judah after the country's division. What were they like? How did they interact with idols and other nations? What were their legacies?

_____

_____

_____

_____

_____

4. How did God provide for Elijah? How have you found the description of the "still small voice" to be true in your life (19:12)?

_____

_____

_____

_____

_____

# 2 Kings

"Thus says the LORD, the God of David your father: 'I have heard your prayer, I have seen your tears; surely I will heal you.'"

2 KINGS 20:5

. . . . . . . . . . . . . . . . . . . . . . . . . . . . .

READING PLAN
9 days; 2.75 chapters a day

THEMES
history of the divided kingdoms; Elijah's death; ministry of Elisha

MAJOR PLAYERS
Ahab, Elijah, Elisha, Jezebel, Naaman, (see also kings chart)

. . . . . . . . . . . . . . . . . . . . . . . . . . . . .

## Background

This continuation of 1 Kings covers approximately two hundred fifty years of Hebrew history, from circa 850 BC to 586 BC, when Jerusalem was burned and the people were either destroyed or sent into exile. It tells of the last twelve kings of the north and the last sixteen kings of the south and corresponds to the book of 2 Chronicles.

## Summary

Second Kings continues the story of the dizzying array of rulers in the northern and southern kingdoms, their reigns, and their many mistakes. The bloody fight against Baalism continued. Elijah was taken to heaven after completing his fight, leaving his ministry to Elisha. While Elijah was a fiery, wild-man prophet, Elisha was gentle and urbane. Most of the miracles recorded in this book are acts of love and mercy. Nevertheless, the crumbling morals and idol worship that saturated both kingdoms led to their downfalls. While David's line no longer sat on a literal throne, it would be continued with Christ.

## Reflections

1. Scholars often drawn parallels between the ministries of Elijah and Elisha and those of John the Baptist and Jesus. From what you have learned about both Old Testament prophets, what do you think of this observation?

_____

_____

_____

_____

_____

2. Contrast Elijah's acts of fire and sword against Baalism and the miracles of mercy from Elisha. Thinking back to the "still small voice" story in 1 Kings 19, how does this reveal how God would prefer to deal with His people?

_____

_____

_____

_____

_____

_____

3. How does 2 Kings reveal the character of God? The character of humankind?

_____

_____

_____

_____

_____

_____

_____

_____

_____

4. Through all the ups and downs of this history of the Hebrew people, what stands out as most remarkable to you? Most confusing? Most inspiring? How is this account like a spiritual history of humankind?

_____

_____

_____

_____

_____

_____

_____

_____

_____

# 1 Chronicles

David said to his son Solomon, "Be strong and of good courage, and do it; do not fear nor be dismayed, for the LORD God—my God—will be with you. He will not leave you nor forsake you, until you have finished all the work for the service of the house of the LORD."

1 CHRONICLES 28:20

. . . . . . . . . . . . . . . . . . . . . . . . . . . . . . . . .

## READING PLAN
11 days; 3 chapters a day

## THEMES
genealogies; David's reign; plans for the temple

## MAJOR PLAYERS
David, Solomon

. . . . . . . . . . . . . . . . . . . . . . . . . . . . . . . . .

## Background

Many of the events in the Chronicles will be familiar, since they cover the same time period as the books of Samuel and the Kings. First Chronicles corresponds with 1 and 2 Samuel. These books do give different details, however, of God's dealings with His people during this time. The books were likely written circa 500 BC to encourage the returned exiles in Jerusalem to make temple worship a more important part of their lives. It's possible that Ezra was the author, but no one knows for sure.

# Summary

Why does this book begin with such lengthy and detailed genealogies? Perhaps because the audience—the remnant of Jews who had returned to Jerusalem after the exile—was living without a king. Still, the line of David was promised to sit on the throne forever, and the promise of the Messiah to revive this line would have brought them hope. You'll also see that David's focus on the temple is covered in great detail, perhaps reminding the people how glorious the first temple had been and how God had been present in its many details. The temple was to be honored.

# Reflections

1. What did you learn from 1 Chronicles that you didn't catch in 1 and 2 Samuel? Why do you think these new details were recorded for us?

   _____

   _____

   _____

   _____

   _____

   _____

   _____

   _____

   _____

2. In a way, this is more of a spiritual history than a straight "chronicle." How did the spiritual example of David have encouraged the exiled Jews to carry on? How does it encourage you?

_____

_____

_____

_____

_____

_____

_____

3. Although God accepted His people's use of the tabernacle, it was David's joy to build a temple. How have you seen God honoring people's attempts to bring Him glory on earth? Why didn't God let David build the temple? What was David's response (1 Chronicles 28)?

_____

_____

_____

_____

_____

_____

_____

_____

4. Think about the details involved in the preparation for the temple, including the assembly of priests, Levites, and all its workers. Clearly, much thought went into the preparation. After reading David's final praise to God, what were the most important things to him about God's house? What might an attitude like this change about our houses of worship today?

_____

_____

_____

_____

_____

_____

_____

_____

_____

_____

_____

_____

_____

_____

_____

_____

_____

_____

# 2 Chronicles

"If My people who are called by My name will humble
themselves, and pray and seek My face, and turn
from their wicked ways, then I will hear from heaven,
and will forgive their sin and heal their land."

2 CHRONICLES 7:14

. . . . . . . . . . . . . . . . . . . . . . . . . . . . .

## READING PLAN
10 days; 3.5 chapters a day

## THEMES
Solomon's reign; history of Judah

## MAJOR PLAYERS
kings of Judah (see previous list), Solomon

. . . . . . . . . . . . . . . . . . . . . . . . . . . . .

## Background

The book of 2 Chronicles corresponds with the events of 1 and
2 Kings. This account, though, focuses completely on Solomon
and the rulers of the southern kingdom of Judah, mentioning the
northern kingdom of Israel only as it relates to the south. Second
Chronicles covers events from Solomon to those surrounding the
Babylonian captivity in 586 BC.

# Summary

In this book you'll receive a different version of the reign of Solomon and the history of Judah. After Solomon's successes and the glory of the temple, Judah's history took a nosedive. The kingdom divided after his death, and so began a line of kings ranging from good to bad to worse. In this book you'll read about their intrigues and reforms. One ruler would set up idols; another would tear them down. Some would try to clean up Judah's act; others would embark on campaigns of evil so dire that God could not withhold punishment. After the north was wiped out and dispersed, the south was left with a surviving remnant who would return to Jerusalem. They needed to know their history—and so do we.

# Reflections

1. What lessons should the returning remnant of Judah have taken away from this account of their national history?

_____

_____

_____

_____

_____

_____

_____

_____

_____

2. What details did you pick up on that were different from the account in 1 and 2 Kings? Why do you think these new details were included for us?

_____

_____

_____

_____

_____

_____

_____

_____

3. See if you can keep track of the rulers, their state with God, and what their reigns were like. Which ruler stands out to you the most? Why?

_____

_____

_____

_____

_____

_____

_____

_____

_____

4. Sum up Israel's history and how it reveals the person of God to us. What are some areas that interest you for further study?

_____

_____

_____

_____

_____

_____

_____

_____

_____

_____

_____

_____

_____

_____

_____

_____

_____

_____

_____

_____

# Ezra

Ezra had prepared his heart to seek the Law of the LORD, and
to do it, and to teach statutes and ordinances in Israel.
EZRA 7:10

. . . . . . . . . . . . . . . . . . . . . . . . . . . . . . .

## READING PLAN
3 days; 3.5 chapters a day

## THEMES
revival; rebuilding; restoration after a period of judgment

## MAJOR PLAYERS
Ezra, Haggai, King Artaxerxes, King Cyrus, King Darius,
Zechariah, Zerubbabel

. . . . . . . . . . . . . . . . . . . . . . . . . . . . .

## Background

This book of spiritual history covers the Jews' return from exile
in Babylon. Tradition tells us that the priest himself, Ezra, wrote
the book, along with 1 and 2 Chronicles and Nehemiah. Written
circa 456–444 BC, the books of Ezra and Nehemiah were likely
one big book.

## Summary

After the fall of Babylon, King Cyrus of Persia allowed
Zerubbabel to take a group of Jews back to Jerusalem to rebuild

their temple, as Isaiah foretold. When they arrived, they praised God, kept feasts, and laid the temple's foundations. But their scheming neighbors managed to stop progress for fifteen years. Haggai and Zechariah urged the people to resume, and King Darius gave his full support and protection until the temple was finished. Approximately sixty years later, a second group of Jews was authorized to return, led by Ezra. But when he arrived, he found the Israelites up to their old habits of intermarriage and idolatry. Ezra enacted harsh reforms, the people repented, and they set about restoring religious life in Jerusalem, showing us how restoration always follows repentance.

## Reflections

1. In the book of Ezra, you can see cycles of mourning and joy, repentance and revival. At one point, the cycles mix poignantly as the old men shout for joy at the laying of the temple's foundations, but weep because it was just a shadow of Solomon's splendid temple (3:12). Have you experienced any times when you mourned what happened but rejoiced in what God brought you through?

_____

_____

_____

2. In exile, God's people likely wondered whether He had abandoned their covenant. In what ways did He work in circumstances and in hearts of men to restore them to their home? How does that give you hope for miraculous restoration?

_____

_____

_____

3. The end of Ezra describes a time of national mourning and confession. In what ways did revival follow reform?

_____

_____

_____

_____

_____

_____

_____

_____

4. Is there an area of your life where you need revival? Does it correspond with an area where you need to repent? Reflect on the ways revival and repentance connect in your own life, and jot down some key verses from Ezra to encourage you on your path.

_____

_____

_____

_____

_____

_____

_____

_____

_____

# Nehemiah

"But if you return to Me, and keep My commandments and do
them, though some of you were cast out to the farthest part of
the heavens, yet I will gather them from there, and bring them
to the place which I have chosen as a dwelling for My name."

NEHEMIAH 1:9

. . . . . . . . . . . . . . . . . . . . . . . . . . . . .

## READING PLAN
6 days; 2 chapters a day

## THEMES
courage; leadership; dedication; restoration of the Jews

## MAJOR PLAYERS
King Artaxerxes, Nehemiah

. . . . . . . . . . . . . . . . . . . . . . . . . . . . .

## Background

This book is written from a first-person perspective, and it
could have been copied from Nehemiah's reports by Ezra or col-
lected by Nehemiah himself. It was written during the reign of
Artaxerxes I (Esther's stepson) circa 464–424 BC. Nehemiah's
text follows the events in Ezra, when Ezra had been in Jerusalem
approximately fourteen years and the temple had been restored.

# Summary

After the temple had been restored and the first two groups of Jews had returned to their homeland, Nehemiah brought a third group to restore the walls of the city. Nehemiah was King Artaxerxes' cupbearer, a trusted associate, and he gained permission to return to his people's ancestral home and make it a fortified city once again. Notice how the group set about work: organized, armed, and bravely focused through opposition. When they finished, Nehemiah and Ezra read from the book of the law and brought about a revival. They dedicated the wall and began another wave of reforms in the Jewish community. God rebuilt not only the walls but also their daily lives.

# Reflections

1. How does the way Nehemiah led the people, and the way they went about their work, inspire you as you face a large or difficult task? What principles can you glean from their approach?

_____

_____

_____

_____

_____

_____

_____

2. Nehemiah was famously a man of prayer. How long did he pray before asking the king's permission to return? In what ways was prayer the real foundation of the walls? How can it be the foundation of whatever you build in your life?

_____

_____

_____

_____

_____

3. In this book we see another cycle of neglecting God's law, and we also witness the rekindling of interest in the law. How does it encourage you to know that the Bible can always be rediscovered? Have you ever experienced, or are you experiencing, revival in your life as a result?

_____

_____

_____

_____

_____

4. When Zerubbabel and Ezra rebuilt the temple, it was obviously a "spiritual" task; Nehemiah's walls required more practical, everyday work. But how were they also an important part of God's plan? What kind of "everyday" work can you rededicate to God?

_____

_____

_____

_____

# Esther

Go, gather all the Jews who are present in Shushan, and fast
for me; neither eat nor drink for three days, night or day.
My maids and I will fast likewise. And so I will go to the
king, which is against the law; and if I perish, I perish!

ESTHER 4:16

. . . . . . . . . . . . . . . . . . . . . . . . . . . . . . .

## READING PLAN
2 days; 5 chapters a day

## THEMES
destiny; duty; God's faithful protection of the Jews

## MAJOR PLAYERS
Ahasuerus, Esther, Haman, Mordecai, Queen Vashti

. . . . . . . . . . . . . . . . . . . . . . . . . . . . . . .

## Background

The events in Esther backtrack approximately thirty years
before Nehemiah, between the years that passed during Ezra
6–7, in the 470s BC. The author of Esther is an unknown
Jewish eyewitness, possibly Mordecai. It was written sometime
after Ahasuerus (Xerxes) died in 465 BC. Thanks to Esther,
the Jews enjoyed enough favor to gain royal support for their
return to Jerusalem.

# Summary

The book of Esther records another escape from annihilation for the Jews, this time because of a brave queen. You'll read about the fall of Vashti, how Esther won a royal contest to become King Ahasuerus of Persia's new wife, and how she risked her life to advocate for her people when they were threatened by an ill-advised royal decree. She and Mordecai exposed the evil Haman and turned the tables on those who plotted to kill the Jews. The king gave the Jews permission to fight back against their enemies, and they beat them soundly, celebrating with the Feast of Purim. Through Esther, God protected His people and set the stage for Jerusalem to be rebuilt.

# Reflections

1. While Esther was worrying about her dilemma, Mordecai advised Esther, "Who knows whether you have come to the kingdom for such a time as this?" (4:14). She had a role to play in history. Do you believe you have a role to play? How would you describe the "such a time as this" that God has placed you in?

   _____

   _____

   _____

   _____

   _____

   _____

   _____

2. Think about the danger involved in approaching the king and how easily Haman and his wise men manipulated him. How different is our situation with God? How does it free you to know that you can approach Him at any time, day or night, and that He is always just?

_____

_____

_____

_____

_____

3. Look at Haman's feud with Mordecai. How did Mordecai handle Haman's venom? What are the differences in their motivations?

_____

_____

_____

_____

_____

4. Esther and Mordecai ended up as queen and prime minister of Persia, and they took many risks to influence ungodly authority for the protection of God's people. Though it may be frightening, how might this encourage you to speak up against harmful policies in our day and age?

_____

_____

_____

_____

# Job

Naked I came from my mother's womb, and naked
shall I return there. The LORD gave, and the LORD has
taken away; blessed be the name of the LORD.

JOB 1:21

. . . . . . . . . . . . . . . . . . . . . . . . . . . . . .

## READING PLAN
13 days; 3.25 chapters a day

## THEMES
mystery of human suffering and pain; God's sovereignty

## MAJOR PLAYERS
Bildad, Elihu, Eliphaz, Job, Job's wife, Zophar

. . . . . . . . . . . . . . . . . . . . . . . . . . . . . .

## Background

Job might be the oldest book in the Bible and may have taken
place around the time of Genesis 11. Its writer is not identified,
but tradition suggests it could be Moses, Job himself, or another
Jew living between 500 BC and 200 BC.

## Summary

With Job, we begin the Bible's books of poetry and wisdom. This
is a historical poem, also called a biblical drama, exploring some
of humanity's deepest and most painful questions: Why do we

suffer? Does God care? Is God just? You'll see how the great man Job was crushed by a series of disasters and how his friends made things worse by trying to explain why he experienced them. Job refused to curse God or to accept responsibility for his suffering—and, in fact, he was not responsible. Finally, Job ran out of words, and God spoke to him, filling him with awe. Job received a revelation, shifted his focus, and repented, and God delivered him and restored double what was taken. The only answer to his suffering was the presence of God Himself.

## Reflections

1. When have you or someone you love struggled to understand suffering? Has anyone tried to explain it the way Job's friends did? What effect did that have?

_____

_____

_____

_____

2. In the great mystery of human suffering and tragedy, how does Job show us how to respond? How can his story help us learn to suffer more honestly and more faithfully, without trying to twist ourselves to make things make sense in our limited worldview?

_____

_____

_____

_____

3. Look at the chapters where Job finally ran out of words to say, and then God spoke. What do they tell us about who God is in relation to our human condition?

_____

_____

_____

_____

_____

_____

4. It's possible that Job never understood the reason he suffered, yet he remained faithful. What statements of his faith can you adopt? How do they apply to your life today?

_____

_____

_____

_____

_____

_____

5. How is seeking the presence of God the only response to suffering? What are the alternatives?

_____

_____

_____

_____

_____

_____

# Psalms

This is the day the LORD has made; we
will rejoice and be glad in it.
PSALM 118:24

. . . . . . . . . . . . . . . . . . . . . . . . . . . . . . . . .

## READING PLAN
28 days; 5 chapters a day

## THEMES
songbook of Israel, covering a full range of human emotions
and faithful expressions

## MAJOR PLAYERS
Asaph, David, Ethan, Moses, sons of Korah

. . . . . . . . . . . . . . . . . . . . . . . . . . . . . . .

## Background

This magnificent book is a treasury of the songs of Israel, covering approximately one thousand years from the time of Moses
all the way through to the end of the Old Testament. Authors
include David (73); Asaph (12); the sons of Korah, or those
descended from Moses' cousin Korah (11); Solomon (2); Moses
(1); Ethan (1); and anonymous writers (50).

# Summary

You are about to spend some quality time with one of the most beloved books of the Bible—the Psalms. These psalms are the highest monument to a great poet-king, David, and a hymnal of songs used in worship throughout Israel's history. Readers have found a staggering breadth and depth of human emotion in these songs; Jesus quoted them often, even while hanging from the cross. Some of them were written especially about Him, the Messiah (2, 8, 16, 22, 45, 69, 72, 89, 110, 118). While we read them as poetry, they were written to be sung.

Psalms can be divided into five books:

Book I: Psalms 1–41
Book II: Psalms 42–72
Book III: Psalms 73–89
Book IV: Psalms 90–106
Book V: Psalms 107–150

This division may have been chosen to mirror the themes in the Pentateuch: I for events in Genesis; II for Exodus; III for Leviticus; IV for Numbers; and V for Deuteronomy.

When you reach book V, you'll find a few significant subgroups. The *Hallel Psalms* (113–118) were traditionally sung on the night of Passover and may have been sung by Jesus and the disciples at the Last Supper. The *Songs of Ascent* (120–134) were pilgrim songs sung by those traveling uphill toward Jerusalem, or possibly while on the stairs to the temple. The *Psalms of Thanksgiving* (135–139) and *Hallelujah Psalms* (146–150) round out a book in heartfelt hymns to God's greatness. As you read, you'll be joining generations who have been brought closer to the knowledge of God through song.

# Reflections

1. Try giving each psalm your own title and summarizing its focus in your own words. Do you identify with it personally? Does it correspond to periods of your own life?

_____

_____

_____

_____

_____

_____

_____

_____

2. As you finish each "book" division, experiment with finding parallel themes in the Pentateuch (for example, songs of creation for Genesis or songs crying for mercy in Exodus). What themes and stories could they be matched up with today?

_____

_____

_____

_____

_____

_____

_____

3. Many of us love the psalms of joy and praise, but there are plenty of psalms about anger, vengeance, devastation, and mourning. How did these affect you, in conjunction with their surrounding songs? What do they portray, and why (for example, psalms of vengeance = a burning thirst for justice, etc.)?

_____

_____

_____

_____

_____

_____

_____

_____

4. As you reflect, identify which psalms you can hold in reserve and use as prayers in your life for the things you pray about most. Which ones speak to you and why?

_____

_____

_____

_____

_____

_____

_____

_____

# Proverbs

The fear of the LORD is the beginning of wisdom,
and the knowledge of the Holy One is understanding.
PROVERBS 9:10

. . . . . . . . . . . . . . . . . . . . . . . . . . . . . .

## READING PLAN
11 days; 3 chapters a day

## THEMES
wisdom for a faithful life

## MAJOR PLAYERS
Agur, Lemuel, Solomon

. . . . . . . . . . . . . . . . . . . . . . . . . . . . . .

## Background

Solomon wrote the bulk of these pithy sayings, although a few
are attributed to Agur and King Lemuel. These writers are
unknown in history and may have been other names for Solomon
himself. The final form of the book is dated circa 700 BC, and
Solomon's original is dated circa 900 BC. Chapters 25–29 are
copied from old manuscripts by Hezekiah's men, two hundred
years after Solomon—possibly because the manuscripts were old
and worn out.

# Summary

Proverbs is a collection of Solomon's wise sayings for living a holy life and avoiding pitfalls. It was written for young men but is useful for anyone and for all ages. Subjects cover the gamut of practical life, with advice on everything from parenting to money management. These are words from the experiences of a human being, but the gist of Solomon's guidance is that following God's commands is wise, and everything else is foolish.

# Reflections

1. What's the best advice you've ever received? Why?

_____

_____

_____

_____

_____

_____

_____

_____

_____

_____

_____

_____

2. Did you read anything in Proverbs that particularly applied to your life? What wisdom applied the most to you?

_____

_____

_____

_____

_____

_____

_____

_____

3. Knowing what you know about Solomon, how did his experiences offer him keen insight? Which stories show you that?

_____

_____

_____

_____

_____

_____

_____

_____

_____

4. If you were going to share godly advice with young people, or even with your younger self, what would it be? Write your own proverbs, and share them with someone in your community.

_____

_____

_____

_____

_____

_____

_____

_____

_____

_____

_____

_____

_____

_____

_____

_____

_____

_____

_____

_____

# Ecclesiastes

To everything there is a season, a time for
every purpose under heaven.

ECCLESIASTES 3:1

. . . . . . . . . . . . . . . . . . . . . . . . . . . . . . . . .

READING PLAN
3 days; 4 chapters a day

THEMES
transience of earthly life; meaninglessness; cycles of life

MAJOR PLAYERS
the Preacher (Solomon)

. . . . . . . . . . . . . . . . . . . . . . . . . . . . . .

## Background

Scholars widely accept Solomon as the author of this book,
though it may have been another writer mimicking his style and
writing from Solomon's viewpoint. If it was Solomon, he was
likely writing wrote circa 930 BC when he had reached old age.

## Summary

Solomon, famous for his wisdom and wealth, had seen and
enjoyed everything "under the sun." (1:14). But all these earthly
things he found lacking. His soul, like ours, longed for things
eternal, and he saw meaninglessness and monotony in things that

should have given him "the good life." While you'll find many proverbs and observations of the human condition in this book, you'll sense beneath them a yearning for true joy—the kind only Christ can bring and the kind Solomon could only hope for in a world that had not yet seen the Messiah. Today, even as we see history repeating itself, we have hope under the sun.

## Reflections

1. When in your life have you longed for something and asked, "Is this all there is?" Did that change your perspective on how to live life?

_____

_____

_____

_____

_____

_____

2. What have you observed to be "vanity" (1:2) and "grasping for the wind" (1:17) when you think of life's pursuits?

_____

_____

_____

_____

_____

_____

3. In Solomon's time, God had not revealed much about His plans for eternity. How does hope for eternal life change an attitude of hopelessness at the transience of this earthly life?

_____

_____

_____

_____

_____

_____

_____

_____

4. If life is a vapor and any earthly inheritance we leave is swept away, what kind of spiritual inheritance do you hope to leave? And to whom? How can you use your life to leave a legacy of God's hope and love?

_____

_____

_____

_____

_____

_____

_____

_____

_____

# Song of Solomon

My beloved spoke, and said to me: "Rise up,
my love, my fair one, and come away."
SONG OF SOLOMON 2:10

. . . . . . . . . . . . . . . . . . . . . . . . . . . . .

## READING PLAN
1 day; 8 chapters a day

## THEMES
romantic human love; devotion and faithfulness; love of God
for His people

## MAJOR PLAYERS
beloved (the king or a shepherd), daughters of Jerusalem
(chorus), Shulamite (the bride)

. . . . . . . . . . . . . . . . . . . . . . . . . . . . .

## Background

Solomon wrote 1,005 songs, but this one is commonly praised
as the loveliest he produced during his reign from 971 BC to
931 BC.

## Summary

This passionate book of poetry describes romantic love in some
fairly steamy metaphors. Aside from a picture of love between
two human lovers, Jews read this book at Passover to explain the

love of God for His people at the Exodus, when He took them away as His own. Christians tend to see these verses as a picture of Christ and His bride, the church. The fact that Solomon had many wives and a large harem has led some to believe that the Shulamite resists the king's advances and holds fast to her shepherd lover, who comes to take her away. However you read it, it's a celebration of the kind of faithful love our hearts are made for.

## Reflections

1. From a romantic standpoint, we see here an intense wooing followed by a return to the Shulamite's home, a marriage, and a "going forth" into life. What does it say to you about God that this kind of love is celebrated as a gift from Him? What keeps us from celebrating love between humans as both a spiritual and a physical experience?

_____

_____

_____

_____

_____

2. Observe when the Shulamite told the maidens not to stir up love until it pleases (8:4). What does "until it pleases" look like? What does mature and faithful love look like?

_____

_____

_____

_____

_____

3. Looking at this as a book about Christ and His church, what strikes you the most about the king's attitude toward the maiden, or Jesus' attitude about toward you? How can you nurture a sense of longing and appreciation like this in your faith?

_____

_____

_____

_____

_____

_____

_____

_____

4. Describe your sense of passion in your life and in your faith. Do you truly believe this passion is available to you and approved by God? Why, or why not?

_____

_____

_____

_____

_____

_____

_____

_____

# Isaiah

For unto us a Child is born, unto us a Son is given; and
the government will be upon His shoulder. And His
name will be called Wonderful, Counselor, Mighty
God, Everlasting Father, Prince of Peace.

ISAIAH 9:6

. . . . . . . . . . . . . . . . . . . . . . . . . . . . . . .

## READING PLAN
15 days; 4.5 chapters a day

## THEMES
prophecies of the Messiah, of Judah's future, and of the new
heavens and new earth

## MAJOR PLAYERS
Ahaz, the Branch (Jesus), Hezekiah, Isaiah, Jotham, Uzziah

. . . . . . . . . . . . . . . . . . . . . . . . . . . . . . .

## Background

Isaiah is the first book of the Prophets in the Bible; from here
on, the Old Testament features books of prophecy. The first five
are considered Major Prophets because of their length, and the
last twelve are the Minor Prophets. Isaiah was the cousin of King
Uzziah and grandson of King Joash, so he would have had clear
access to kings and leaders. His ministry lasted from circa 740
BC to 700 BC.

# Summary

Prophets in the Old Testament did more than hear from God; they were often advisors to kings. Isaiah was an advisor to kings Uzziah, Jotham, Ahaz, and Hezekiah in Judah. Throughout Isaiah's life, Judah had been threatened by Assyria, which had its capital in Nineveh. Assyria indeed wiped out the nation of Israel—the northern kingdom. As you read, you'll notice how Isaiah shifts back and forth from matters of war and state, to specific and rhapsodic prophecies about the coming Messiah and the new heaven and new earth. You might recognize many words in Isaiah from Handel's *Messiah* and other Christmas traditions because he predicted the Christ child so completely—including the virgin birth, nativity, His eventual suffering, and His victory over death. Isaiah spoke some of the most beautiful words in the Bible about humankind's need for salvation—and God's promise and provision of it.

# Reflections

1. Keep track of when Isaiah shifts from visions of the near future (the rise and fall of nations) to the far future (the Messiah and His final reign). What do you observe? Why would that combination have been important to the people he prophesied to?

   _____

   _____

   _____

   _____

   _____

2. Write down the information Isaiah gives about the Messiah.
   What does it say about God's character? Refer back to this
   information when you reach the Gospels.

   _____

   _____

   _____

   _____

   _____

   _____

   _____

   _____

   _____

3. What does the book of Isaiah have to say about fear and peace?
   Collect verses as you go, and reflect on what bearing they
   might have on the fears you face today.

   _____

   _____

   _____

   _____

   _____

   _____

   _____

   _____

   _____

   _____

4. At the time of Isaiah's ministry, Judah worshipped with their mouths, but not fully with their hearts and their obedience. What words from Isaiah can lead you deeper into a more authentic devotion and inspire you to identify and leave behind a more surface-level religion?

# Jeremiah

"I know the thoughts that I think toward you, says the
LORD, thoughts of peace and not of evil, to give you a future
and a hope. Then you will call upon Me and go and pray
to Me, and I will listen to you. And you will seek Me and
find Me, when you search for Me with all your heart."
JEREMIAH 29:11–13

## READING PLAN
16 days; 3.25 chapters a day

## THEMES
Jerusalem's final chance to repent; prophecies and history of the
fall of Jerusalem

## MAJOR PLAYERS
Ahikam, Baruch, Jehoiachin, Jehoiakim, Jeremiah, Zedekiah

## Background

Jeremiah prophesied approximately one hundred years after
Isaiah. While Isaiah focused on the coming Assyrians, Jeremiah
warned of the coming Babylonians. Jeremiah started his work
circa 626 BC and prophesied for forty years. Jeremiah didn't
write his scroll in chronological order; it was jotted down as he
dictated it to his secretary, Baruch—so you may want to consult
other clarifying resources.

# Summary

In this book you'll find out why Jeremiah is called "the weeping prophet," mourning, begging, pleading, and sobbing over the stubbornness of God's people. God gave them one last chance to repent and turn back from idolatry, which had grown so bad that they were offering human sacrifices and worshipping foreign gods. Alas, they refused. Heartbroken, Jeremiah prophesied that if they would submit to the coming Babylonians, they would be partly spared. But the people ridiculed and persecuted him for this unpatriotic idea. Still, Jeremiah looked forward to the day when, as God told him, Judah would be lifted to power and Babylon would be destroyed.

In this book you'll read a mixture of prophecy, history, and personal accounts of Jeremiah's fraught relationships with the leaders and people to whom he ministered. He faced opposition, mocking, public humiliation, and even prison and assassination attempts, yet he could only keep repeating his message, each time with more feeling: God's people were running toward their own ruin. Yet with equal feeling, he looked forward to the day when the old covenant, which the people had broken, would be replaced by a new covenant. Restoration was coming.

# Reflections

1. Keep track of the times Jeremiah and God pleaded with the people to return to Him. How does it affect you to know that God was as heartbroken as Jeremiah when His people turned from Him? And that He still offered a future and a hope (29:11)?

_____

_____

_____

_____

_____

_____

_____

2. Keep track of the judgments made against God's people and surrounding nations. What was the gist of their wrongdoing?

_____

_____

_____

_____

_____

_____

_____

_____

3. God called Jeremiah to give a perennially unpopular message, and he was openly upset about the coming wrath. As upsetting as the punishment was, what reasons were given for it?

_____

_____

_____

_____

_____

_____

_____

_____

4. Keep an eye out for Jeremiah's raw pleading for understanding. What do you notice about it? Do you mourn over events in this world or find them impossible to understand? How can you come before God with more honesty, seeking Him with all your heart?

_____

_____

_____

_____

_____

_____

_____

_____

_____

# Lamentations

Through the LORD's mercies we are not consumed,
because His compassions fail not. They are new
every morning; great is Your faithfulness.

LAMENTATIONS 3:22–23

. . . . . . . . . . . . . . . . . . . . . . . . . . . . . . . . .

## READING PLAN
2 days; 2.5 chapters a day

## THEMES
grief over the destruction of Jerusalem; sin and suffering; hope
for restoration

## MAJOR PLAYERS
Jeremiah (prophet), Zion / Jerusalem

. . . . . . . . . . . . . . . . . . . . . . . . . . . . . . . . .

## Background

Jeremiah's prophecies came true: Nebuchadnezzar destroyed
Jerusalem in 586 BC, and the people went into exile. This short
poem was written in grief, set as an acrostic to the Hebrew alphabet,
likely so it could be distributed and memorized among the exiled.

## Summary

Jeremiah, the weeping prophet, mourned the fall of Jerusalem
in this short lament. Zion had sinned, and they were now faced

the horrific consequences he'd warned them of. God was angry and seemed far from them. Through their misery, though, came repentance—which subsequently led to prayer, hope, and restoration. Despite crushing ruin, because he knew the character of God, Jeremiah had hope that He would bring them out of desolation. Indeed, Jerusalem would later be restored.

## Reflections

1. Why was this an important text for those in exile? What do you think was the purpose of each chapter?

_____

_____

_____

_____

_____

_____

2. Describe the contrast between the first and last half of chapter three. How did Jeremiah know the Lord would draw near?

_____

_____

_____

_____

_____

3. Jeremiah did not downplay, excuse, or place blame on anyone but Zion for their fate. What does this book teach us about what sincere lament and repentance look like?

_____

_____

_____

_____

_____

_____

_____

_____

_____

4. How do we tend to downplay the suffering that comes as a consequence of sin? How can we be more honest in our laments before God, and how can we be more hopeful of His mercies?

_____

_____

_____

_____

_____

_____

_____

_____

# Ezekiel

> He said to me, "Prophesy to these bones, and say to
> them, 'O dry bones, hear the word of the LORD! Thus
> says the Lord GOD to these bones: "Surely I will cause
> breath to enter into you, and you shall live."'
>
> EZEKIEL 37:4–5

. . . . . . . . . . . . . . . . . . . . . . . . . . . . . .

## READING PLAN
16 days; 3 chapters a day

## THEMES
comforting the exiles; visions and symbolic actions about the
destruction and restoration of Israel

## MAJOR PLAYERS
Ezekiel ("son of man"), Jehoiachin, Zedekiah

. . . . . . . . . . . . . . . . . . . . . . . . . . . . . .

## Background

After the northern kingdom of Israel was sent into exile by
Assyria, the southern kingdom fell to Babylon in three stages:
the first wave of exiles was captured in 605 BC (with Daniel), the
second wave was taken in 597 BC (with Ezekiel), and finally the
capital Jerusalem was burned in 586 BC. So Ezekiel was writing
to his fellow exiles. He wrote from 593 BC to 571 BC, starting
at age thirty. This heavily symbolic book is often considered one
of the most difficult to understand in the Bible, so have some
supplemental materials handy as you journal.

# Summary

Ezekiel spoke with actions and words, painting a vivid and dramatic picture for the exiles: Jerusalem and its neighbors would fall, but God would care for and restore His people. They wouldn't get to go home as they hoped, but in the meantime, they would come to know without a doubt that God is God and He is sovereign. Ezekiel's prophecy comes in three parts: first, judgment of the Israelites' sins and the destruction of Jerusalem; second, the destruction of their neighbors; and third, the restoration and reunion of the people, including the coming of the Spirit, the coming of Christ, and His spectacular future reign on earth.

You'll read about Ezekiel's prophetic *actions:* in his silence, he was committing to speak only what God commanded; in baking bread over excrement, he gave a sign of famine due to their sins; in lying on his side, he acted out their discomfort; in shaving his hair and scattering it to the wind, he predicted how God's people would be scattered. You'll also read of his prophetic *visions,* many of which you'll see again in the book of Revelation. Ezekiel also told prophetic *parables,* describing the sins of the people and their consequences. The prophet acted as a watchman, calling out to the people what was on the horizon. After destruction would come a rebuilt temple and Christ's river flowing with the water of life, streaming out into the whole world and bringing life where there had only been dry bones before.

# Reflections

1. Keep track of Ezekiel's prophetic *actions*, as directed by God. Though they may seem strange to us, how were they especially effective to those who witnessed them?

_____

_____

_____

_____

_____

_____

_____

_____

2. Write down a list of Ezekiel's colorful prophetic *visions*. Whom were they for? What did they mean? Which ones stand out to you the most?

_____

_____

_____

_____

_____

_____

_____

_____

3. Consider the *parables* Ezekiel told. Why might storytelling have been the best option for the subjects he addressed?

_____

_____

_____

_____

_____

_____

_____

_____

4. In a vision, Ezekiel ate a scroll (3:3)—and so did John, the writer of Revelation (Revelation 10:10). They both had to ingest and fully digest the Word of God before hearing from Him and speaking to the people. How have you begun to digest God's Word more fully though the practice of journaling? How has it affected you? Where would you like to improve?

_____

_____

_____

_____

_____

_____

_____

# Daniel

So Daniel was taken up out of the den, and no injury whatever was found on him, because he believed in his God.

DANIEL 6:23

. . . . . . . . . . . . . . . . . . . . . . . . . . . . . . .

## READING PLAN
4 days; 3 chapters a day

## THEMES
God's miraculous appearances in Babylon; Daniel's prophecies for the end of the world

## MAJOR PLAYERS
Abed-Nego, Belshazzar, Daniel, Darius, Meshach, Nebuchadnezzar, Shadrach

. . . . . . . . . . . . . . . . . . . . . . . . . . . . . . .

## Background

Daniel was both a prophet and a statesman in Babylon. Tradition tells us that he wrote this book circa 530 BC, as a very old man. The first half details his miraculous adventures, and the second is prophecy.

## Summary

The first half of Daniel recounts how God appeared miraculously for him during his captivity in Babylon: in the interpretation of dreams, for his friends in the fiery furnace, in the famous lions' den, and in reading the "writing on the wall." God made Himself known as the one and only God, even among the Gentile kings and nobles. One king after another bowed to Him. The second half of Daniel, written in his old age, is a different style altogether. You'll want to read it closely with a good commentary to truly understand the layers of his prophecies, many of which correspond with Revelation's accounts of the end times, the rise and fall of kingdoms, and the appearance of the Messiah and events yet to come. Take time to dig in, and as the book of Matthew says about Daniel, "Whoever reads, let him understand" (24:15).

## Reflections

1. Through Daniel and his friends, God showed Himself powerful time after time. What did each of His miracles say about Him to the Gentiles in Babylon, where many Jews were exiled?

_____

_____

_____

_____

2. The fourth man in the furnace is commonly considered to be Jesus (3:25). Where does Jesus appear in the first and the last half of this book? In what roles does He reveal Himself?

_____

_____

_____

_____

3. Did your study of chapters Daniel 7–12 reveal anything surprising to you about events to come? In what ways would this have given hope to Jews in exile? In what ways does it give hope to Christians today?

_____

_____

_____

_____

_____

_____

4. God displayed His glory in the events of Daniel's life, and He gave glimpses of His coming glory in Daniel's prophecies. Throughout the rise and fall of world powers, how does the knowledge that God will be glorified affect the way you speak and act? How can you begin to behave more like Daniel did as he served under rulers who did not know God?

_____

_____

_____

_____

_____

_____

_____

_____

# Hosea

Hear the word of the LORD, You children of Israel, for the
LORD brings a charge against the inhabitants of the land:
"There is no truth or mercy or knowledge of God in the land."

. . . . . . . . . . . . . . . . . . . . . . . . . . . . . . . . . .

## READING PLAN
2 days; 7 chapters a day

## THEMES
fidelity versus adultery; God buying back people who had
betrayed Him

## MAJOR PLAYERS
Gomer, Hosea, Jezreel, Lo-Ammi, Lo-Ruhamah, northern
kingdom of Israel (a.k.a. Ephraim, Jacob, Samaria)

. . . . . . . . . . . . . . . . . . . . . . . . . . . . . . . . . .

## Background

Hosea was a prophet mostly to the northern kingdom of Israel.
He wrote this book likely after their capital fell, circa 722–721
BC. Before Hosea, God had sent Elijah, Elisha, Jonah, and
Amos to warn the people to return to Him.

# Summary

Hosea's life was a living parable of how God chases after and redeems a people who are unfaithful to Him over and over. God instructed Hosea to marry Gomer, an unfaithful wife who cheated on him repeatedly. Though Hosea was devastated by this treatment, he had three children with her, and he even bought her back on the open market after she had wandered astray. God used this story to show His people how heartbroken He was that they had forgotten and betrayed Him with other gods and how willing He was to restore them if they would truly turn to Him.

# Reflections

1. Hosea 4:6 says the people perished for lack of knowledge. Not only did their priests and prophets not guide God's people, but the people actively rejected God. How can you commit to gaining knowledge of God and acting on it? How can you help or encourage your community to pursue this knowledge?

_____

_____

_____

_____

_____

_____

_____

2. Just as Gomer would stray and reconcile, but not really mean it, Israel would offer God lip service and not really mean it. In Hosea 6:6, what did God ask the people for? What does God prefer rather than demonstrative acts of remorse?

_____

_____

_____

_____

_____

3. Have you witnessed or experienced the devastating effects of infidelity in human relationships? What does it mean to you that God feels these effects and that He will always pursue His people?

_____

_____

_____

_____

_____

4. In what ways did the people act out their infidelity against God? In what modern ways do we face idolatry, and in what ways do we excuse idolatry?

_____

_____

_____

_____

_____

_____

# Joel

"I will pour out My Spirit on all flesh; your sons and
your daughters shall prophesy, your old men shall
dream dreams, your young men shall see visions."

JOEL 2:28

. . . . . . . . . . . . . . . . . . . . . . . . . . . . . . . . . . .

READING PLAN
1 day; 3 chapters a day

THEMES
coming judgment; the day of the Lord; predicting the day of
Pentecost

MAJOR PLAYERS
Joel, son of Pethuel

. . . . . . . . . . . . . . . . . . . . . . . . . . . . . . . . . . .

## Background

Sadly we don't know much about the prophet Joel, and there are
very few clues about the time the book was written. It's widely
considered to be an early book of prophecy, circa 830–750 BC,
and written to the southern kingdom of Judah.

## Summary

In Joel you'll see a vivid account of coming judgment, both
in invasion from the north and in the final end times and the

second coming of Christ. God foreshadowed His judgment through a plague of locust that destroyed the crops. Enemies would come like locusts, but God would restore what the locusts had eaten. Joel also predicted the outpouring of the Holy Spirit in Acts 2, making Joel the "prophet of Pentecost." Joel laid out, yet again, the pattern of desolation and deliverance of God's people as seen in the other prophets.

## Reflections

1. In chapter 1, what effect do the locusts have on the people and their worship? Where do they go for shelter?

_____

_____

_____

_____

_____

_____

2. Do you give much thought to the "day of the Lord" (2:1) or the return of Christ? How does the thought of this event affect people—for better or for worse? What did Joel say is the way to prepare for this?

_____

_____

_____

_____

_____

_____

3. In chapter 2, Joel told the people to return to God with fasting and repentance. How and why should we make "returning to the Lord" a regular practice until He returns to us on earth?

_____

_____

_____

_____

_____

_____

_____

4. The book of Acts refers to Joel 2:28, when the Spirit is poured out. In Joel's context, it is also connected to "the "great and awesome day of the LORD" (v. 31). How have you witnessed His Spirit poured out in your life?

_____

_____

_____

_____

_____

_____

_____

_____

# Amos

"But let justice run down like water, and
righteousness like a mighty stream."

AMOS 5:24

. . . . . . . . . . . . . . . . . . . . . . . . . . . . . .

## READING PLAN
2 days; 4.5 chapters a day

## THEMES
predicting exile and captivity; consequences of corruption

## MAJOR PLAYERS
Amaziah, Amos, Israel (northern kingdom), Judah (southern
kingdom)

. . . . . . . . . . . . . . . . . . . . . . . . . . . . . .

## Background

Amos was not a priest or a noble, but a layman prophet—a sheep
breeder and an arborist for sycamore trees. He was from the
southern kingdom of Judah, with a message for the northern
kingdom of Israel and its neighbors, writing circa 750 BC.

## Summary

The kingdom of Israel was successful and prosperous, but not all
was well. An immoral, rich ruling class oppressed the poor, and
sin ran rampant. Amos prophesied around the same time as Joel

and Hosea, and he warned that the scales had tipped toward disaster. He likened God's people to a bowl of fruit that was just about to go rotten and warned that consequences were inevitable (Amos 8). Disaster was coming to them and to the surrounding nations, but God would save and restore a remnant. Sure enough, thirty years later, the kingdom fell and a remnant was taken into exile.

## Reflections

1. Amos had a lot to say to the people who had grown used to luxury and overindulgence and who cruelly took advantage of the wealth disparity in the kingdom for corrupt ends. How can we act to make sure that we, as individuals and as a society, aren't guilty of the same kind of mindset?

_____

_____

_____

_____

_____

2. In what ways was the priest Amaziah complicit with the particular failings of the people? How can Christians avoid this today?

_____

_____

_____

_____

_____

3. What effect do you think Amos's credentials (or lack of them) had on the fashionable people he was speaking to? Have you experienced God speaking His truth through unsophisticated means? What was the effect on the listeners?

_____

_____

_____

_____

_____

_____

_____

_____

4. In what areas do you see justice and righteousness lacking in the treatment of the poor and vulnerable? How can you act and pray that God's justice will rain down and that what is broken may be made right?

_____

_____

_____

_____

_____

_____

_____

_____

# Obadiah

And the kingdom shall be the LORD's.
OBADIAH V. 21

. . . . . . . . . . . . . . . . . . . . . . . . . . . . . . . .

## READING PLAN
½ day; 1 chapter a day; read with Jonah

## THEMES
prophesied destruction of the Edomites, Israel's longtime
enemies; God's dedication to defending His people

## MAJOR PLAYERS
Edomites (descendants of Esau), Israel (a.k.a. house of Jacob),
Obadiah

. . . . . . . . . . . . . . . . . . . . . . . . . . . .

## Background

This book of prophecy is the shortest book in the Old Testament.
While it may be tempting to skim through it, take some extra
time to flip back to your notes on Genesis and review the story
of Jacob and Esau before you begin Obadiah (Genesis 25).

There are at least twelve Obadiahs in the Old Testament,
and this prophet could be any of them, or none. That's why
scholars find it difficult to date the writing of this text. Some
say 570 BC, or much earlier, circa 848–841 BC. The earlier
date would make Obadiah a contemporary of Elisha. Either
way, this brief, fiery book illustrates God's commitment to His
people, Israel.

# Summary

Edom had treated Israel cruelly, betraying them when they were under attack and refusing to come to their aid. To make matters worse, Edom seemed to have it all. The kingdom was located near the Red Sea and was blessed with good land and the beautiful city of Petra. The Edomites looted others and brought the spoils home. They'd gotten away with it for a long time, but their crass celebration of Jerusalem's defeat was a step too far. God sent Obadiah to tell the Edomites that their cruelty would see them wiped out. Thanks to Obadiah's prophecy, Israel could have hope that they wouldn't be downtrodden forever and could know that their enemies would see God's justice.

# Reflections

1. Review the story of Jacob and Esau. What thoughts do you have about the historical conflict in Obadiah? How does it inform your reading of Obadiah?

   _____

   _____

   _____

   _____

   _____

   _____

   _____

   _____

2. How does cruelty and lack of compassion between groups of people rear its ugly head today? What does it accomplish?

_____

_____

_____

_____

_____

_____

3. What does God's reaction toward a wealthy nation who refused to help His downtrodden, war-battered people teach us today?

_____

_____

_____

_____

_____

4. How can we, as individuals and as a nation, become more compassionate toward others, knowing that God's justice will be served?

_____

_____

_____

_____

_____

# Jonah

"Should I not pity Nineveh, that great city, in which are more than one hundred and twenty thousand persons who cannot discern between their right hand and their left—and much livestock?"

JONAH 4:11

. . . . . . . . . . . . . . . . . . . . . . . . . . . . . .

## READING PLAN
½ day; 4 chapters a day; read with Obadiah

## THEMES
God's love for all people; obedience; repentance; forgiveness

## MAJOR PLAYERS
Jonah, Ninevites, one big fish

. . . . . . . . . . . . . . . . . . . . . . . . . . . . . .

## Background

This book is technically anonymous, but Jonah likely wrote it. He was a prophet from Galilee during the reign of Jeroboam II (793–753 BC). Jesus would use Jonah's three days in the fish as an illustration of His coming resurrection.

## Summary

Nineveh was the capital of Assyria, which was in the process of cruelly crushing and taking over the northern kingdom of Israel. So when God called Jonah to speak to them, it must have felt like treason. He fled in a boat as far as he could in the opposite direction, but he was thrown overboard and swallowed by the famous fish. When he was coughed up on land, Jonah accepted God's call and preached to the Ninevites, who later repented and were saved. Irritated, Jonah complained, but God showed him how much He wished for all people to be saved through repentance.

## Reflections

1. What has been your experience in praying for your enemies? How would you feel if God blessed them?

   _____

   _____

   _____

   _____

2. Think of Jonah's experience with the vine (Jonah 4). When do you tend to struggle with the idea that people are more important than things?

   _____

   _____

   _____

3. How does the parallel between Jesus going into the tomb for three days and Jonah being in the fish for three days inform your concept of what He did for us? (Hint: we are the Ninevites in this situation.)

   _____

   _____

   _____

# Micah

He has shown you, O man, what is good; and what
does the LORD require of you but to do justly, to love
mercy, and to walk humbly with your God?

MICAH 6:8

. . . . . . . . . . . . . . . . . . . . . . . . . . . . . . . . . .

## READING PLAN
1 day; 7 chapters a day

## THEMES
predicting consequences for Judah and Israel; predicting
Christ's birth and the hope of His kingdom

## MAJOR PLAYERS
Israel (northern kingdom), Judah (southern kingdom), Micah

. . . . . . . . . . . . . . . . . . . . . . . . . . . . . .

## Background

Micah was a prophet from Judah in the south, circa 740–687 BC.
He prophesied for two good kings (Jotham and Hezekiah) and
one evil one (Ahaz).

## Summary

God's people hadn't listened to Elijah, Elisha, or Amos, so
God sent Micah to repeat to the Jewish capitals, Jerusalem and
Samaria, that He was coming to judge their wickedness. The

rich still abused the poor, religion was meaningless, and God would bring His justice to them. But Micah also predicts the day when Jesus would come and rule the earth, as well as sets the stage for the Messiah to be born in Bethlehem, and he also predicted the day when Jesus would come and rule the earth. After the suffering would come indescribable glory.

## Reflections

1. What was the state of religious life as Micah described it? How did they gloss over serious issues? How are similar issues glossed over today?

_____

_____

_____

_____

_____

2. The people offered meaningless sacrifices, still going about their business without a change of heart. We might not offer animals or food as sacrifices, but we do tend to offer "sacrifices" to please God, like time, activity, and resources. How can we make sure what we do "for God" is done with our hearts in the right place and undergirded with justice, mercy, and humility?

_____

_____

_____

_____

_____

3. When Micah asked, "Who is a God like You?" (7:18), how did he describe God? What does this book teach us about God in relation to His people?

_____

_____

_____

_____

_____

_____

_____

_____

4. Micah made a stark comparison between the earthly kingdom and the coming kingdom. What are those differences? How can we prepare for this coming kingdom?

_____

_____

_____

_____

_____

_____

_____

_____

# Nahum

The LORD is good, a stronghold in the day of trouble;
and He knows those who trust in Him.

NAHUM 1:7

. . . . . . . . . . . . . . . . . . . . . . . . . . . . . . .

READING PLAN
1 day; 3 chapters a day

THEMES
end of Nineveh and judgment of the Assyrians

MAJOR PLAYERS
king of Assyria, Nahum, Ninevites

. . . . . . . . . . . . . . . . . . . . . . . . . . . . . .

## Background

We don't know much about Nahum, except he was from the town of Elkosh in Galilee. He wrote between 663 BC and 612 BC and was the second minor prophet to speak to Nineveh, after Jonah.

## Summary

God had spared Nineveh, the Assyrian capital, when they responded to Jonah's message, but their repentance did not last. They returned to cruel military practices and scorned God. So Nahum was sent to prophesy their doom—and this time it would stick. Their stranglehold on God's people would break, and they would be fully destroyed. Indeed, Nineveh fell to Babylon in 612 BC, approximately one hundred fifty years after Jonah, and the site was not rediscovered until the nineteenth century.

## Reflections

1. What are the key ways Nahum described God's character in this book? How did he illustrate these ways?

_____

_____

_____

_____

2. How was bad news for Nineveh good news for everyone else who cried out to God?

_____

_____

_____

_____

3. Though the Ninevites had once turned to God, they had come to trust in their own might and wealth, and it led to disaster. How can we look for the ways we trust in our own power rather than in God's?

_____

_____

_____

_____

# Habakkuk

"Behold the proud, his soul is not upright in
him; but the just shall live by his faith."

HABAKKUK 2:4

. . . . . . . . . . . . . . . . . . . . . . . . . . . . . . . . . . . . . . .

## READING PLAN
½ day; 3 chapters a day; read with Zephaniah

## THEMES
choosing faith and optimism over doubt and despair

## MAJOR PLAYERS
Chaldeans (a.k.a. Babylonians), Habakkuk, King
Nebuchadnezzar

. . . . . . . . . . . . . . . . . . . . . . . . . . . . . . . . . . .

## Background

We know little about Habakkuk himself, and the book is difficult to date, but it's assumed to have been written circa 625–606
BC. Judah had been wicked, and the Babylonians were on their
way to destroy them.

## Summary

Habakkuk had some complaints and questions for God. If moral
conditions in Judah were bad, Babylon was worse. It didn't make
sense that God would use them to mete out just punishment to

His people. But God replied that He was ultimately about the business of justice. Habakkuk prayed and praised God for His power and care and concluded that he could only respond with faith and rejoicing, even though the enemy was closing in. God was still God, and He still cared for His people.

## Reflections

1. Habakkuk openly questioned God. How can asking honest questions help grow and strengthen our relationship with Him?

_____

_____

2. At the beginning of chapter 2, Habakkuk says he will "set [himself] on the rampart" to watch and wait for God's guidance and correction (v. 1). How can you prioritize quiet watching and waiting for God in your daily life?

_____

_____

3. How would you characterize Habakkuk's prayer and hymn prayer (3:1–16) in chapter 3? How would a prayer remembering God's great works in your life be read?

_____

_____

_____

4. Habakkuk 3:17–19 is a powerful statement of faith. How can you grow in yourself a similar attitude in times of want and fear?

_____

_____

# Zephaniah

"The LORD your God in your midst, the Mighty One, will
save; He will rejoice over you with gladness, He will quiet
you with His love, He will rejoice over you with singing."

ZEPHANIAH 3:17

. . . . . . . . . . . . . . . . . . . . . . . . . . . . .

## READING PLAN
½ day; 3 chapters a day; read with Habakkuk

## THEMES
day of judgment; coming restoration

## MAJOR PLAYERS
Zephaniah

. . . . . . . . . . . . . . . . . . . . . . . . . . . . .

## Background

Zephaniah was the great-great-grandson of King Hezekiah and
a contemporary of the king of Judah in his day, Josiah. He wrote
not long before the Babylonians destroyed Jerusalem in 586 BC,
likely circa 621–612 BC.

## Summary

Zephaniah announced the day of God's wrath when, as long
predicted, the Babylonians would sweep across the land and
dominate the Israelites as well as their neighbors just twenty

years later. But God would, He assured, judge righteously, and a remnant would be saved and restored. Zephaniah referenced the end times as well, and he looked forward with rejoicing to the day all would be healed and made right. For all the darkness, even more light would come.

## Reflections

1. From reading this book, how are God's wrath and His love are connected? Why did He have to judge the Israelites? The citizens of Judah?

_____

_____

_____

_____

2. What do you find most remarkable about the contrast of darkness and light in this book? How could the love and joy in the second half still occur in light of the destruction of the first half?

_____

_____

_____

3. Have you ever struggled to believe in God's love during a time of suffering? How could the message in this book speak to that situation?

_____

_____

_____

# Haggai

Then Haggai, the LORD's messenger, spoke the LORD's message
to the people, saying, "I am with you, says the LORD."

HAGGAI 1:13

. . . . . . . . . . . . . . . . . . . . . . . . . . . .

## READING PLAN
1 day; 2 chapters a day

## THEMES
rebuilding the temple; strength; fortitude

## MAJOR PLAYERS
Haggai, Zerubbabel

. . . . . . . . . . . . . . . . . . . . . . . . . . . .

## Background

Haggai is the first of the post-exile prophets, speaking to the
Jews after their return to Jerusalem. The book was written in
520 BC, the second year of King Darius of Babylon. After the
book of Obadiah, Haggai is the next shortest book in the Old
Testament—but we'll spend a day with it, also reacquainting ourselves with the other Old Testament books written during this
time period: Ezra, Nehemiah, and Esther.

## Summary

Haggai ministered to the first group of Jews to return to
Jerusalem, led by Zerubbabel. (See Ezra.) At the time of his

writing, construction on the temple had stalled for fifteen years. The people had made themselves quite comfortable and neglected God's call to rebuild. A drought followed, and Haggai pointed out that God would send rain and provide for them if they got back to work on God's house. They jumped to it, and Haggai encouraged and guided them with God's words, promising a glorious temple to come not just then but in the end times.

## Reflections

1. It can be easy to see to our own comfort and to neglect God's house, the church. What are some ways you can recommit to this task?

_____

_____

2. Haggai promised that God would provide for those who worked on His temple by ending the drought. What keeps you from trusting that God will bless you for doing His work?

_____

_____

3. Haggai said that good work doesn't make an unclean worker clean; the priest had to go into a task with holiness (2:10–14). How can we ensure that we go about our work for God with a holy heart and mind?

_____

_____

4. How does the end of the book describe Zerubbabel as a "type" or symbol of the coming Messiah, Jesus?

_____

_____

# Zechariah

"For who has despised the day of small things? For these seven rejoice to see the plumb line in the hand of Zerubbabel."

ZECHARIAH 4:10

. . . . . . . . . . . . . . . . . . . . . . . . . . . . . .

## READING PLAN
2 days; 7 chapters a day

## THEMES
encouraging the rebuilders of the temple; predicting the Messiah's life, death, and work

## MAJOR PLAYERS
the Branch (Messiah), Joshua (the high priest), Zechariah, Zerubbabel

. . . . . . . . . . . . . . . . . . . . . . . . . . . . . .

## Background

Zechariah lived at the same time as Haggai, and he took over Haggai's ministry of encouraging the remnant to rebuild the temple. His ministry overlaps Ezra 5 and started in 520 BC.

## Summary

Zerubbabel had brought the remnant of Jews back from exile to start rebuilding, but the people were discouraged. It was going slow and looking unimpressive. So God sent Zechariah to join Haggai in encouraging the people with visions of Israel's magnificent future. Things wouldn't be like this forever. The New Testament quotes Zechariah approximately forty times because it speaks so vividly about the Messiah—with details about His birth, life, crucifixion, and coming again in glory. The remnant's "small" job was just the beginning of a new heaven and a new earth to come.

## Reflections

1. What does it mean to you personally that even the most important things start small? What small work in your life have you been tempted to "despise"?

_____

_____

2. Investigate the role of the Branch in this book. How did Jesus fulfill all these prophecies?

_____

_____

3. What information from Zechariah can you use to crystalize in your mind the work Jesus did on earth?

_____

_____

_____

4. If you were a craftsman and your life were your craft, what in this book would you find most encouraging as you went about your tasks for God's glory?

_____

_____

# Malachi

"Behold, I send My messenger, and he will prepare the way before Me. And the Lord, whom you seek, will suddenly come to His temple."

MALACHI 3:1

. . . . . . . . . . . . . . . . . . . . . . . . . . . .

## READING PLAN
1 day; 4 chapters a day

## THEMES
God's final words to His people in the Old Testament; serving God faithfully

## MAJOR PLAYERS
Malachi, messenger (John the Baptist), Sun of Righteousness (Messiah)

. . . . . . . . . . . . . . . . . . . . . . . . . . . .

## Background

This last prophet of the post-exile period is also the last recorded prophecy for the four hundred years between the Old and New Testaments. Malachi's dates are unclear, but estimates say he was writing circa 470–450 BC.

## Summary

The Israelites had been back in Jerusalem for approximately one hundred years and, repeated old patterns, and drifted away from

God. Malachi came to shake them out of their apathy and lazy spiritual practices. He aimed to inspire them to serve God faithfully through tithes, proper sacrifices, and holy living and leadership. If they didn't believe it, he said, they could wait and see. Something big was coming. God had set in action the coming of the Messiah and the final day of the Lord.

## Reflections

1. Think about how these words must have echoed as the last ones spoken directly from God to His people for four hundred years. What do you see as the most important points?

   _____

   _____

2. Malachi pleaded against the spiritual lethargy of the people. When have you experienced or witnessed spiritual lethargy? What kinds of activities manifested during this time? What, if anything, stopped the lethargy?

   _____

   _____

3. What is your approach to monetary generosity in your life? How do Malachi's points about tithing speak to you?

   _____

   _____

4. The people waited several hundred years for the Messiah after this book was written, and Christians wait now for Him to come again. What can you learn from Malachi in your waiting period?

   _____

   _____

# New Testament

# Matthew

"Do not think that I came to destroy the Law or the
Prophets. I did not come to destroy but to fulfill."

MATTHEW 5:17

. . . . . . . . . . . . . . . . . . . . . . . . . . . . . .

## READING PLAN
13 days; 2.25 chapters a day

## THEMES
gospel of Jesus Christ; His role as Anointed One

## MAJOR PLAYERS
Andrew, Barabbas, Bartholomew (Nathanael), Caiaphas,
Herod, James son of Alphaeus, James son of Zebedee, Jesus,
John son of Zebedee, John the Baptist, Joseph, Judas Iscariot,
Judas son of James (Thaddaeus), Mary, Mary Magdalene,
Matthew (Levi), Philip, Pilate, Simon Peter (Cephas), Simon
the Zealot, Thomas, wise men

. . . . . . . . . . . . . . . . . . . . . . . . . . . . . .

## Background

This first Gospel by Matthew serves as a bridge between the Old
and New Testaments and the four hundred years that had passed
between them. Matthew, also known as Levi, was a tax collector
and used to keeping detailed records. He focused on a mainly
Jewish audience and is thought to have written the Gospel first
in Hebrew, and then it was translated to Greek, the lingua franca
of the day, circa AD 60.

# Summary

Here in the Gospels, you've reached the climax of the Bible's story—the coming of Christ and salvation of humankind. You will read four different accounts, aimed at four different audiences, but each with the same message: Jesus is the Messiah, He has come to save us, and He will come again.

The book of Matthew may not be the first Gospel written chronologically, but this organized, easy-to-follow account makes an ideal transition and introduction to the life of Christ. Matthew wrote to the Jews to assure them that Jesus was the One promised by the Old Testament. Starting with a genealogy reaching back to Abraham, Matthew placed Jesus in the context of history. He frequently used quotes and imagery from the Old Testament, focusing on what would have been most important to the Jews as they asked themselves, "Who is Jesus?"

Matthew presented the Sermon on the Mount as parallel to the Ten Commandments in the Old Testament, and he focused heavily on the idea of the kingdom of God. The Jews expected an earthly, political kingdom that would free them from Roman rule, but God had something bigger in mind. Jesus came to reign in the hearts of people for all time, as individuals, as people groups, in the church, in the world, and in heaven. He's freed us of our sins and revolutionized the old way of relating with God. And now that we've received the good news, we can watch and wait with hope for His return.

# Reflections

1. In what ways did Matthew set Jesus firmly in the context of the Old Testament? What parallels did he draw? What proofs did he offer of Jesus being the Messiah that would have spoken to the Jews?

_____

_____

_____

_____

_____

_____

2. The Pharisees (who believed in the Law and the Prophets), Sadducees (who believed only in the Law), and teachers of the Law had built a complex culture around keeping the Mosaic law and protecting it from Greek and Roman influence. Put yourself in the listeners' shoes. What kind of relief must believing Jews have felt at Jesus' revolutionary pronouncements? Why was there some resistance to accepting Him?

_____

_____

_____

_____

_____

_____

_____

3. Compare the Ten Commandments (Exodus 20) and the Sermon on the Mount (Matthew 5–7), as well as the Beatitudes (Matthew 5:1–12). What do you notice? In what ways did Jesus come to fulfill, not destroy, the Law and Prophets?

_____

_____

_____

_____

_____

_____

4. What did Jesus teach about the kingdom of heaven? What about His kingdom on earth? How does this teaching affect you?

_____

_____

_____

_____

_____

_____

5. What parts of Matthew's Gospel stand out to you most? Why?

_____

_____

_____

_____

_____

_____

# Mark

"Even the Son of Man did not come to be served, but
to serve, and to give His life a ransom for many."

MARK 10:45

. . . . . . . . . . . . . . . . . . . . . . . . . . . . . . . .

## READING PLAN
8 days; 2 chapters a day

## THEMES
Gospel according to Mark; miracles, deity, and servanthood
of Jesus

## MAJOR PLAYERS
Andrew, Bartholomew (Nathanael), Herod, Herodians, Jairus,
James son of Alphaeus, James son of Zebedee, Jesus, John
son of Zebedee, John the Baptist, Joseph of Arimathea, Judas
Iscariot, Judas son of James (Thaddaeus), Mary Magdalene,
Matthew (Levi), Pharisees, Philip, Pilate, Simon of Cyrene,
Simon Peter (Cephas), Simon the Zealot, Thomas

. . . . . . . . . . . . . . . . . . . . . . . . . . . . . . . .

## Background

John Mark was a young follower of Jesus and close associate of
Peter. It's believed that he recorded many of Peter's memories of
Christ in his Gospel. John Mark was later an attendant of Paul
and Barnabas in the book of Acts and possibly the "certain young
man" who fled naked from Jesus' arrest in Mark 14:51. While
this Gospel is difficult to date, it's widely accepted to have been
written in Rome circa AD 57–60.

# Summary

The shortest Gospel, Mark, focuses on the acts, miracles, and deity of Christ for a Roman audience. Compact and dynamic, the book focuses more on Jesus' actions than His words. You'll see extensive accounts of healings, cleansings, miracles, and supernatural power, as well as a simple introduction to the Christian faith. It's possible that since young Mark acted as an attendant or servant, he had a particular eye toward the servanthood of Christ—and the specific beauty of our powerful God appearing on earth as a suffering servant.

# Reflections

1. What stands out to you most about this short account? If you were a first-century Gentile, would this Gospel have convinced you of the godhood of Jesus Christ?

   _____

   _____

   _____

   _____

2. Keeping track of the miracles Mark described, reflect on what they say about the personality and attitude of God toward His people.

   _____

   _____

   _____

   _____

3. What convinced the disciples of Jesus' deity? What has convinced you?

_____

_____

_____

_____

_____

_____

_____

_____

_____

_____

4. Reflect on Jesus' role as the perfect servant, though He was God in the flesh. What does that stir within you? How does it inform your actions and your faith practice?

_____

_____

_____

_____

_____

_____

_____

_____

_____

_____

# Luke

She brought forth her firstborn Son, and wrapped
Him in swaddling cloths, and laid Him in a manger,
because there was no room for them in the inn.

LUKE 2:7

. . . . . . . . . . . . . . . . . . . . . . . . . . . .

## READING PLAN
12 days; 2 chapters a day

## THEMES
Jesus' humanity and kindness; prayer and praise

## MAJOR PLAYERS
Andrew, angels, shepherds, wise men, Anna, Bartholomew
(Nathanael), Caesar Augustus, Cleopas, Elizabeth, Gabriel,
Herod, James son of Alphaeus, James son of Zebedee, Jesus,
John son of Zebedee, John the Baptist, Joseph, Judas Iscariot,
Judas son of James (Thaddaeus), Mary, Mary Magdalene,
Joanna, Mary mother of James, Matthew (Levi) , Philip,
Pilate, Simeon, Simon Peter (Cephas), Simon the Zealot,
Theophilus, Thomas, Zacharias

. . . . . . . . . . . . . . . . . . . . . . . . . . . .

## Background

Luke, a physician, is the only Gentile writer in the Bible. He
was from Antioch, and he was a companion of Paul. More
scientific and research-minded, Luke would have carefully col-
lected firsthand accounts to present to Theophilus, probably

a Roman official to whom Luke wrote. Luke likely wrote the Gospel in the early AD 60s. The book of Acts is a sequel to the book of Luke.

## Summary

Luke wrote to an audience immersed in Greco-Roman culture that would have looked for the perfect example of a divine human, so he emphasized both Jesus' humanity and His flawlessness. Here you'll read many examples of Jesus' compassion, kindness, and outreach to the many broken, messy, needy humans He encountered in all social classes and situations. Luke wanted to point out that Jesus was fully human *and* divine, so it's thought Luke met Jesus' mother, Mary, to compile the most complete account of Jesus' birth, much of which we read each year at Christmastime.

You will see Jesus grow up and embark on His ministry, training His disciples and confronting very human problems such as greed, selfishness, pride, the love of money, and the many struggles that affect the human heart. You'll also see particular attention given to the class divisions people faced during that time, as well as a focus on women and children. As you read of the way Jesus trained His disciples to face the world and the way He confronted assumptions and pretenses, you'll find that life hasn't changed all that much—and Jesus' message is just as needed today.

# Reflections

1. Jesus is God, but He still prayed as naturally as He breathed. Observe Jesus' prayers and when, why, and how He prayed. How can His approach to prayer broaden yours?

_____

_____

_____

_____

_____

_____

_____

2. Jesus talked in a no-nonsense way about prioritizing God in your relationships with your family and with other people. Is anything you read difficult to accept? What is the "cost of discipleship," (9:57–62) and how and why must we pay it (9:57)?

_____

_____

_____

_____

_____

_____

_____

3. Which of Jesus' acts of compassion impacts you the most? Why? How can you make that kind of compassion a part of your life?

_____

_____

_____

_____

_____

_____

_____

_____

_____

4. What is your experience with the Golden Rule (6:31)? How did Jesus describe it, and why is it difficult to practice?

_____

_____

_____

_____

_____

_____

_____

_____

_____

# John

In the beginning was the Word, and the Word was with
God, and the Word was God. He was in the beginning
with God. All things were made through Him, and
without Him nothing was made that was made.

JOHN 1:1–3

. . . . . . . . . . . . . . . . . . . . . . . . . . . . . .

## READING PLAN
9 days; 2 chapters a day

## THEMES
Jesus is God; God's message to us

## MAJOR PLAYERS
Andrew, Bartholomew (Nathanael), Caiaphas, James son
of Alphaeus, James son of Zebedee, Jesus, John son of
Zebedee, John the Baptist, Judas Iscariot, Judas son of James
(Thaddaeus), Mary Magdalene, Mary, Martha, and Lazarus of
Bethany, Mary mother of Jesus, Matthew (Levi), Nicodemus,
Philip, Pilate, Simon Peter (Cephas), Simon the Zealot,
Thomas, woman at the well

. . . . . . . . . . . . . . . . . . . . . . . . . . . . . .

## Background

The first three Gospels are called the *Synoptic* Gospels, which
means essentially "seen together." They have a lot of similarities
and may have informed one another. The Gospel of John is in a
different category—the apostle John wrote much later (circa AD

90–95) and was intent on writing a "spiritual gospel" to verify to the upcoming second generation that these events occurred. His aim was also to verify to them that Jesus is indeed God. The apostle John was likely a teenager when he began to follow Jesus, but he wrote this and now, writing this final Gospel, he was an old man with mature powers of reflection. John was one of Jesus' inner circle of disciples, also known as "the disciple whom Jesus loved" (21:20); he had special insight into the eternal meaning of Christ's time on earth. John also may have been Jesus' cousin; he followed John the Baptist as a disciple before being called by Jesus.

## Summary

John revealed that he wrote so "that you may believe that Jesus is the Christ" (20:31) to a new generation that was slowly losing the opportunity to speak with eyewitnesses as their elders passed away. John was wholeheartedly focused on the divinity of Jesus—the fact that He is God. His book is organized around seven signs or miracles that reveal this divinity and is focused on Jesus as the Source of life and hope. It is a beloved Gospel for this reason and many others, including the "gospel in a nutshell" presented in its most famous verse, 3:16.

## Reflections

1. Look out for Jesus' "I am" statements in John. Who did He say He is? Who did His disciples say He is? Who do you say He is?

_____

_____

_____

2. Keep track of the seven signs or miracles John is structured around. What do each of these signs say about God the Father, Son, and Spirit? What do these signs reveal about how they think of us?

_____

_____

_____

_____

_____

3. How did Jesus act as both the Good Shepherd (10:7–30) and Lamb of God (1:29–31) in this book? What significance did that imagery have to the people in John's time? To you?

_____

_____

_____

_____

_____

4. In your journey through the Gospels, how have you found each one to be different? The same? Which one spoke the most to you? Why?

_____

_____

_____

_____

_____

_____

# Acts

"But you shall receive power when the Holy Spirit has come upon you; and you shall be witnesses to Me in Jerusalem, and in all Judea and Samaria, and to the end of the earth."

ACTS 1:8

. . . . . . . . . . . . . . . . . . . . . . . . . . . . . . .

## READING PLAN
11 days; 2.5 chapters a day

## THEMES
birth of the church; life of Paul; the gospel spreads to the Gentiles

## MAJOR PLAYERS
Aquila, Barnabas, Cornelius, Gamaliel, James, Luke, Paul (Saul of Tarsus), Peter, Philip, Priscilla, Silas, Stephen

. . . . . . . . . . . . . . . . . . . . . . . . . . . . . . .

## Background

Acts was written as a sequel to the Gospel of Luke, presumably by the physician Luke himself. He addressed the account to the same Theophilus, a Roman official, and continued in the same style. Luke traveled with Paul and likely wrote the book circa AD 60 or AD 61, while Paul was under house arrest in Rome. This book provides a bridge from the Gospels to the Epistles, telling us the remarkable story of how the faith caught fire in the thirty-three years it covers.

# Summary

The Acts of the Apostles focuses mainly on the work of Peter and Paul—Peter in the first twelve chapters, and Paul in the remaining chapters. You'll read about Jesus' final appearances on earth, His ascension into heaven, and the birth of the church on the day of Pentecost, when the Holy Spirit came upon the disciples as promised. Luke had a historian's eye for details, and he covered the spread of faith in Jesus as thousands were saved across the known world. God continually showed up with miraculous events, healings, and interventions, protecting the fledgling church and making way for the news of Jesus Christ to be spread far and wide—not just to the Jews but to the Gentiles too. You'll read about Paul's conversion, his ministry, and his missionary journeys during his thirty years of ministry. It was a time that truly changed the course of history; the events you're about to read are the reason we know about Christ today.

# Reflections

1. Keep track of the precarious times when all could have been lost and when the early church could have been snuffed out. Does it offer you a new perspective on where we are today?

_____

_____

_____

_____

_____

_____

2. What did God do to keep the church going? What were the miracles, encounters, and support provided that made the most difference? What does that tell you of His attitude toward the church? His love for the church?

_____

_____

_____

_____

_____

_____

_____

_____

_____

3. What is most striking about Peter's words and his ministry in Acts? About his emphasis on the resurrection? How would you respond if you had been in his audience?

_____

_____

_____

_____

_____

_____

_____

_____

4. What resonates with you most about Paul's life, suffering, and journeys in Acts? What kept Paul going, and how do you have access to the same power?

_____

_____

_____

_____

_____

_____

_____

_____

_____

_____

_____

_____

_____

_____

_____

_____

_____

_____

_____

_____

_____

_____

# Romans

I am persuaded that neither death nor life, nor angels nor
principalities nor powers, nor things present nor things to come,
nor height nor depth, nor any other created thing, shall be able to
separate us from the love of God which is in Christ Jesus our Lord.

ROMANS 8:38–39

. . . . . . . . . . . . . . . . . . . . . . . . . . . . . .

## READING PLAN
5 days; 3.25 chapters a day

## THEMES
answering questions regarding what the gospel is, why we need
it, and how we live it

## MAJOR PLAYERS
leaders in the Roman church, Paul, Roman Gentiles, Roman
Jews

. . . . . . . . . . . . . . . . . . . . . . . . . . . . . .

## Background

Paul wrote from Corinth circa AD 56, in the midst of his missionary journeys there. He was worried he might be killed before
he could reach Rome to meet this group. He wasn't—he made it
three years later. He wanted to write to his Roman friends and
address the key truths of the gospel, and he always aimed to
answer their most burning questions.

# Summary

This first epistle, or letter, in the Bible was not the first written chronologically, but it's considered "the head" of the Epistles because it perfectly crystalizes the nature of the gospel. The church in Rome was a mix of Jews and Gentiles. The Jews wondered, "How do we deal with Gentiles who are now part of our faith? Should they be circumcised and act according to our traditions? What do we do with the Law?" Paul pointed out that Jews and Gentiles are all sinners in the same boat, all subject to judgment, and all offered the free gift of grace through Christ. Jesus circumcises the heart—the most important thing—and that changes our very nature. Our works reflect Christ's grace; the Law is there to show us where we've gone wrong. Jesus' free gift of love didn't just land in our laps; the whole of history and the Old Testament led up to this point. And now Jesus' gospel equips us and gives us hope, peace, and perseverance in this life. Now we live as a community, a body of Christ, transformed, bestowed with gifts, and reflecting His love in the world. Our job as a church is to build up one another and give thanks to Jesus with our lives.

As you read Romans, take time to digest this straightforward account of what it means to be redeemed and what it means to be the church today.

# Reflections

1. Based on how Paul described the gospel, what do you think are the most important points? What is repeated often? How would *you* concisely explain the gospel to someone struggling to understand it today?

   _____

   _____

2. What is your experience of living by the Law versus living by Jesus' grace? In what ways do you find yourself trying to earn God's grace or salvation? How do Paul's words here offer you relief?

_____

_____

_____

_____

3. Several key concepts occur in Paul's description of Jesus' work on the cross. What do they both mean in the text and, and what do they mean to you personally? Consider using references to dig into these terms: *grace, redemption, propitiation, justification.*

_____

_____

_____

_____

4. Toward the end of Romans, Paul gives us a beautiful and encouraging picture of a life transformed by Jesus' grace. What does a transformed life look like in your actions? In our relationships with others? In the church? In our communities? In your relationship with the Holy Spirit? In the world at large?

_____

_____

_____

_____

# 1 Corinthians

Now abide faith, hope, love, these three;
but the greatest of these is love.

1 CORINTHIANS 13:13

. . . . . . . . . . . . . . . . . . . . . . . . . . . . .

## READING PLAN
5 days; 3 chapters a day

## THEMES
problems in the church; spiritual gifts; nature of love;
importance of the resurrection

## MAJOR PLAYERS
Apollos, Cephas (Peter), church at Corinth, Paul

. . . . . . . . . . . . . . . . . . . . . . . . . . . . .

## Background

Three years had passed since Paul last visited the church he
founded in Corinth, and the people fell prey to the cultural
vices of the area—a prosperous and luxurious shipping city that
worshipped Aphrodite and was influenced by philosophies of
nearby Athens. So Paul wrote to them from Ephesus circa AD
55, urging them to address their issues and remember that they
were part of something bigger and more wonderful than any one
faction could lay claim to.

# Summary

The Corinthian church comprised many smaller home churches, and they'd started forming cliques, choosing opposing leaders and dividing over issues of doctrine and philosophy. Paul wrote to remind them that the church belongs to God and there is no place for arrogant boasting. The message of Christ is too big for that. As you read, you'll see him address personal issues of morality and call out behavior that was culturally disruptive in that particular church. You'll also read beloved passages on spiritual gifts, the "love chapter," and the importance of the resurrection. It's a reminder to keep priorities where they belong: centered on Christ.

# Reflections

1. Does anything about how the church behaved sound familiar to you? How do you see disunity in the church? When do you see unity like Paul described?

   _____

   _____

   _____

   _____

2. How did the Corinthians blend in too much with the culture around them? How did Paul call them to be separated? How does his advice still ring true today?

   _____

   _____

   _____

   _____

3. What spiritual gifts did Paul highlight, and how are they to be used for the good of all in the body of Christ? What spiritual gifts do you have, and how do you use them for good? (If you haven't explored this, take some time to find online assessments and see what you discover.)

_____

_____

_____

_____

_____

_____

_____

_____

4. When you read the "love chapter," (1 Corinthians 13) note that it comes directly after the exposition on gifts (1 Corinthians 12). How do gifts connect to love, as Paul described it? How does love power gifts?

_____

_____

_____

_____

_____

_____

_____

# 2 Corinthians

Therefore, if anyone is in Christ, he is a new creation; old things
have passed away; behold, all things have become new.

2 CORINTHIANS 5:17

. . . . . . . . . . . . . . . . . . . . . . . . . . . . . . . . . .

## READING PLAN
3 days; 4 chapters a day

## THEMES
defense of Paul's ministry

## MAJOR PLAYERS
Paul, Timothy, Titus

. . . . . . . . . . . . . . . . . . . . . . . . . . . . . . . . . .

## Background

Soon after he wrote his first letter to the Corinthians, Paul felt
anxious to find out how they were doing, so Titus brought him
an update. While the members took some things to heart, certain people led a revolt against Paul's leadership and discounted
everything he had done. Agitated and heartbroken, Paul wrote
to them again circa AD 57 to answer their charges.

## Summary

Here we read a very personal letter, filled with obvious anguish,
written to a church that Paul loved. If the Corinthian church

wanted to know what right Paul had to say such things to them, to lead and pastor them, he was going to tell them about his many sufferings and yet also about the joy and strength God had given him throughout. He had been through extraordinary pain, but his message—Christ's message—and God's glory surpassed it all.

## Reflections

1. Look back to Acts and review some of the events Paul described in his list of sufferings (11:22–33). How was it possible for him to keep going?

---

---

---

---

---

---

2. How has suffering impacted you in the past? How can studying Paul's life and teachings help prepare you for more suffering?

---

---

---

---

---

---

---

3. Paul talked about the thorn in his flesh (possibly a problem with his eyes; 2 Corinthians 12:7-10). What recurring problem could God be calling you to turn to Him for?

_____

_____

_____

_____

_____

_____

_____

_____

4. Why did Paul boast in his weakness? How was this a revolutionary concept? How might it be considered revolutionary thinking today as well?

_____

_____

_____

_____

_____

_____

_____

_____

_____

# Galatians

Stand fast therefore in the liberty by which Christ has made us
free, and do not be entangled again with a yoke of bondage.

GALATIANS 5:1

. . . . . . . . . . . . . . . . . . . . . . . . . . . . . . .

## READING PLAN
2 days; 3 chapters a day

## THEMES
salvation by grace, the Law

## MAJOR PLAYERS
church of Galatia, Judaizers, Paul, Peter, Titus

. . . . . . . . . . . . . . . . . . . . . . . . . . .

## Background

Paul had founded the churches in Galatia several years prior
(circa AD 45–48), and they enthusiastically accepted the gospel. But circa AD 57, he received word that a group called the
Judaizers was teaching the Galatians that they were required to
become Jews before accepting Christ and required to keep Jewish
laws and feasts. Paul wrote this letter to set them straight.

## Summary

Until the fall of the temple in Jerusalem in AD 70, Christianity
was widely considered a sect of Judaism. One group, the Judaizers,

tried to convince enthusiastic new believers that they had to be circumcised in order to be saved and that they had to keep the detailed tenets of Jewish law. The Galatians were pulled into this idea, as was, it seems, the apostle Peter. But Paul was adamant that the new covenant came to replace Abraham's, that this was a faith for the whole world, and that the gospel of grace—given, not earned—surpassed all forms of legalistic bondage.

## Reflections

1. What is the essence of Christ's gospel, according to Paul?

_____

_____

_____

_____

_____

_____

2. How did the people add to (and detract from) that essence? What are some ways modern religious groups do the same?

_____

_____

_____

_____

_____

_____

3. Have you ever had a difficult time leaving behind a misconception? You're in good company—Peter did too. What misconception or earlier belief did you struggle to let go of? How did turning to God and seeking guidance help you?

_____

_____

_____

_____

_____

_____

_____

_____

4. What makes it so difficult to leave traditions that don't serve us or the gospel? Why is it important to do so?

_____

_____

_____

_____

_____

_____

_____

_____

_____

# Ephesians

By grace you have been saved through faith,
and that not of yourselves; it is the gift of God,
not of works, lest anyone should boast.

. . . . . . . . . . . . . . . . . . . . . . . . . . . . . .

## READING PLAN
2 days; 3 chapters a day

## THEMES
mystery of grace; church unity; armor of God

## MAJOR PLAYERS
church at Ephesus, Paul, Tychicus

. . . . . . . . . . . . . . . . . . . . . . . . . . . . . .

## Background

Paul wrote to the Ephesian church while he was imprisoned, likely in Rome, circa AD 60. He wrote a handful of letters at once and sent them all with Tychicus, probably to be circulated around the region. He wrote to a church composed mostly of Gentile believers in an area known for the worship of the goddess Diana.

## Summary

The early church saw much division between Jewish and Gentile believers. This pained Paul, who was adamant about the unity and equality of church members under Christ—for the whole world. In this letter, Paul spoke of the mystery of grace and the spiritual world, of God's purposes for reconciliation, and of God's love for His church. He also covered practical concerns on how to be a unified community, and he gave his classic image of the armor of God for our protection and defense.

## Reflections

1. How comfortable are you with the mysteries of faith? What does Paul teach regarding this subject?

_____

_____

_____

_____

_____

_____

2. What did Paul tell us about the supernatural nature of the "new man" and about spiritual gifts? How are we empowered to change and thrive under Christ? How have you been empowered?

_____

_____

_____

_____

_____

_____

3. Paul encouraged followers to walk in love, light, and wisdom. How would this have made the Ephesians different from their fellow citizens? How does it make us different?

_____

_____

_____

_____

_____

_____

_____

_____

_____

4. Study the "whole armor of God" (6:11). How can you "take it up" every day? How can you be more aware of the spiritual world around you?

_____

_____

_____

_____

_____

_____

_____

_____

_____

# Philippians

The peace of God, which surpasses all understanding, will
guard your hearts and minds through Christ Jesus.

PHILIPPIANS 4:7

· · · · · · · · · · · · · · · · · · · · · · · · · · · · · ·

## READING PLAN
1 day; 4 chapters a day

## THEMES
joy; humility; hope in suffering

## MAJOR PLAYERS
church at Philippi, Epaphroditus, Paul, Timothy

· · · · · · · · · · · · · · · · · · · · · · · · · · · · · ·

## Background

You can read about Paul's founding of the Philippian church in
Acts 16, along with the memorable incident where God miraculously freed Paul and Silas from prison there. Ten years later, while
imprisoned in Rome, Paul wrote them a thank-you letter for their
support, circa AD 61. The Philippian church was the first church
in Europe, and Luke was likely its pastor for some time.

## Summary

On principle, Paul made a point not to accept payment for his
missionary work. He made money as a tentmaker. But in this

case, while he was imprisoned and unable to earn, this beloved community sent a messenger with monetary support. Paul over-flowed with gratefulness and encouragement because the church suffered—they were suffering from persecution as well. But he told them, as he tells us, that incredible joy is possible in both good times and bad, thanks to Jesus.

## Reflections

1. Why is this book nicknamed the "epistle of joy"? How does it encourage you to find joy during difficult times?

_____

_____

_____

_____

_____

_____

_____

2. How is humility important to surviving suffering well? How is it tied to joy?

_____

_____

_____

_____

_____

_____

3. How did the Philippians participate in Paul's ministry?

_____

_____

_____

_____

_____

_____

_____

_____

_____

4. Think of the ways you provide (or would like to provide) support for good works around the world. How can you make this a regular part of your life?

_____

_____

_____

_____

_____

_____

_____

_____

_____

_____

# Colossians

God willed to make known what are the riches of the glory of this mystery among the Gentiles: which is Christ in you, the hope of glory.

COLOSSIANS 1:27

. . . . . . . . . . . . . . . . . . . . . . . . . . . . .

## READING PLAN
1 day; 4 chapters

## THEMES
Christ is God; Christ is sufficient

## MAJOR PLAYERS
Archippus, Epaphras, Paul

. . . . . . . . . . . . . . . . . . . . . . . . . . . . .

## Background

We're unsure whether Paul personally visited the church at Colossae, but he certainly knew their founder, Epaphras, and two of their members, Philemon and Onesimus (more on that later). In this letter from prison in Rome (circa AD 60), Paul addressed some of the worries Epaphras had about the Colossian church, and he reinforced Christ's deity.

## Summary

Apparently the church in Colossae came under the influence of worrying philosophies. False teachers had told them that they had to worship angels instead of approaching Christ directly, and they were also told they had to comply with strict Jewish rules. Some promoted asceticism or self-punishment, and some promoted cutting loose morally. But Paul wrote to clarify that Jesus is God—in them—and the only One to be worshipped; He is truth, and He can't be crammed into a small set of rules. Christ is the source, the Head of the church, and the focus—nothing else.

## Reflections

1. Have you had any run-ins with a brand of faith that focused mainly on philosophy, on legalism, or on the exciting possibilities of the spiritual realms rather than knowing Christ? What was that like? How are we disempowered by centering faith on these things?

_____

_____

_____

_____

_____

2. What does "Christ in you" (1:27) mean to you?

_____

_____

_____

_____

_____

3. What did it mean to the readers in Colossae, and what does it mean to us, that we can approach Christ directly? How do we respond to this privilege?

_____

_____

_____

_____

_____

_____

_____

_____

_____

4. Keep track of Paul's statements about who and what Christ is. Of all the things Christ is, what resonates with you most from this book?

_____

_____

_____

_____

_____

_____

_____

_____

# 1 Thessalonians

If we believe that Jesus died and rose
again, even so God will bring with
Him those who sleep in Jesus.

1 THESSALONIANS 4:14

. . . . . . . . . . . . . . . . . . . . . . . . . . . . .

## READING PLAN
1 day; 5 chapters a day

## THEMES
Jesus' second coming; what happens after death; what to do
while we wait for Jesus

## MAJOR PLAYERS
church at Thessalonica, Paul, Silas, Timothy

. . . . . . . . . . . . . . . . . . . . . . . . . . . . .

## Background

Jumping back in time, we have Paul's earliest existing letter,
believed to have been written circa AD 51. Paul had founded
the church in Thessalonica shortly before, but they ran him out
of town after only a few months. This letter was to continue the
Thessalonians' instruction and answer questions about death and
the coming of Jesus.

## Summary

Paul had been chased out of Thessalonica by those who feared he wished to depose Caesar and replace him with a king named Jesus. Paul felt concerned about this infant church, so he waited eagerly for news—which Timothy brought him. The church was being persecuted, and some members had died. So the believers wondered: What happened with the dead in relation to Jesus' second coming? When will that be? Also, when would Jesus return? Paul wrote to encourage, instruct, and answer these questions to this brave congregation so that they could keep the faith during terrible circumstances.

## Reflections

1. How does Paul's message give comfort and hope to those facing death? How does it give you hope?

_____

_____

_____

_____

_____

_____

_____

_____

_____

_____

2. Paul addressed how the Thessalonians should behave and prioritize while they waited for Jesus' return. What did he advise? How can we do the same?

_____

_____

_____

_____

_____

3. Christ's second coming seemed so immediate to the early church. This believe had both good and unintended consequences. What would change today if you were equally expectant? How should we wait?

_____

_____

_____

_____

_____

_____

4. What were the Thessalonians doing right? How can you, too, walk worthy of the calling you've received?

_____

_____

_____

_____

_____

_____

# 2 Thessalonians

But the Lord is faithful, who will establish
you and guard you from the evil one.

2 Thessalonians 3:3

. . . . . . . . . . . . . . . . . . . . . . . . . . . . . .

## READING PLAN
1 day; 3 chapters a day

## THEMES
more on Jesus' return; the end times

## MAJOR PLAYERS
church at Thessalonica, Paul, Silas, Timothy

. . . . . . . . . . . . . . . . . . . . . . . . . . . .

## Background

Paul wrote this letter very soon after 1 Thessalonians, possibly months or even weeks, circa AD 50 or AD 51. Paul had received word that the Thessalonian church was troubled by inaccurate teachings, and he set out to delve deeper into the topics he addressed in his first letter.

## Summary

The Thessalonians were worried. Had the day of the Lord already come? Paul wrote to tell them what had been revealed to him, a time period known as "the apostasy" (2:3), which would happen before Jesus returned. It had not happened yet and, to our knowledge, still has not. Paul promised that on the day of Jesus' return, justice will prevail and judgment will come for those who had persecuted God's people. The Thessalonians also struggled with members who had given up working in preparation of Jesus' coming and were sponging off others. Paul set them straight with his instructions on work.

*Reflections*

1. How, in your experience, are fear and idleness connected? What did Paul advise about idleness?

_____

_____

_____

_____

_____

_____

2. How did the Thessalonians continue to react to persecution? How was Paul's message designed to keep them growing under pressure?

_____

_____

_____

_____

_____

_____

3. The people faced a lot of confusing ideas from false teachers versus real teachers—and in the end times, Paul said, there will be a false church led by the "man of sin" (2:3). How do we tell the false from the real? How did they?

_____

_____

_____

_____

_____

_____

_____

_____

4. What stands out to you the most from these two letters to the Thessalonians? Why?

_____

_____

_____

_____

_____

_____

_____

_____

_____

_____

# 1 Timothy

Let no one despise your youth, but be an example to the believers
in word, in conduct, in love, in spirit, in faith, in purity. Till I
come, give attention to reading, to exhortation, to doctrine.

1 TIMOTHY 4:12–13

. . . . . . . . . . . . . . . . . . . . . . . . . . . . . . . .

## READING PLAN
1 day; 6 chapters a day

## THEMES
instructions to Timothy on how to care for the church

## MAJOR PLAYERS
church at Ephesus, Paul, Timothy

. . . . . . . . . . . . . . . . . . . . . . . . . . . . . . . .

## Background

Timothy was Paul's spiritual son, and he had been tasked with
guiding the church at Ephesus, the largest Christian church in
the world at the time. Paul wrote to him between AD 64 and
AD 66 with instructions on the work he was to do.

## Summary

You may recognize Timothy's name from Paul's other letters and
from Acts; Timothy was one of Paul's closest confidants, and
Paul was priming the young man for leadership. The church

at Ephesus was actually many small house churches (they had no buildings yet) run by many pastors; they needed to refocus on the most essential and practical points if the church was to survive threats of false teachings from the inside and persecution from the outside. These words on responsibility and church organization still guide churches today.

## Reflections

1. Research more about the culture of Ephesus at the time in Paul's day. How did his instructions tailored to the issues they facing?

---

---

---

---

---

---

---

2. Sum up Paul's standards for leadership. How do you see this happening or not happening today?

---

---

---

---

---

---

3. In this chapter Paul laid down specific guidelines for behavior within the church at Ephesus, especially for women, which are hotly debated still today. Read a variety of trusted, credentialed scholarly sources on these ideas. What do you believe? Why?

_____

_____

_____

_____

_____

_____

_____

_____

4. What has been your experience in leadership? What is the best experience you've had with others' leadership? How do Paul's principles connect with your experience?

_____

_____

_____

_____

_____

_____

_____

_____

_____

# 2 Timothy

For this reason I also suffer these things; nevertheless
I am not ashamed, for I know whom I have believed
and am persuaded that He is able to keep what
I have committed to Him until that Day.

. . . . . . . . . . . . . . . . . . . . . . . . . . . . . .

## READING PLAN
1 day; 4 chapters a day

## THEMES
Paul's last words to Timothy; instructions to stand strong

## MAJOR PLAYERS
Luke, Mark, Paul, Timothy, Titus

. . . . . . . . . . . . . . . . . . . . . . . . . . . . . .

## Background

This is Paul's last known letter, written close to the time of his death by execution in Rome, circa AD 67 or AD 68. Paul wrote it to Timothy, following up on his first letter, and filled it with final and urgent guidance. It's unknown whether Timothy made it back to see Paul, but clearly Paul thought about carrying on his ministry until the end.

# Summary

Paul was in prison in Rome, prosecuted by Nero's court. Christians were widely blamed for the fire that had ravaged Rome, and it's possible these were the charges against him. Paul knew his outlook was grim, so he wrote urgently to Timothy about false teachings invading the church, individual responsibilities, and what Timothy should hold fast to in the coming difficult days. It was a dangerous time to be a Christian, and many, like Paul, faced death and persecution. But Paul knew he had fought well, and he urged Timothy to stand strong in faith.

# Reflections

1. How did Paul advise Timothy to behave while things seemed to be falling apart? How can we commit to similar integrity when things seem to be falling down today?

   _____

   _____

   _____

   _____

2. Knowing what you know about Paul's ministry, how do his final words relate to his life's work and to his priorities in spreading the gospel? What about his ministry and letters resonates the most with you?

   _____

   _____

   _____

   _____

3. What is an approved worker (2:15)? According to Paul, what constitutes good work for Christ?

_____

_____

_____

_____

_____

_____

_____

_____

_____

_____

4. What did Paul say about the Word of God in this book? How might this inform your approach to journaling through the Bible?

_____

_____

_____

_____

_____

_____

_____

_____

# Titus

This is a faithful saying, and these things I want you
to affirm constantly, that those who have believed in
God should be careful to maintain good works.

TITUS 3:8

. . . . . . . . . . . . . . . . . . . . . . . . . . . . . . .

## READING PLAN
½ day; 3 chapters a day; read with Philemon

## THEMES
church leadership in Crete; value of living a good life

## MAJOR PLAYERS
Paul, Titus

. . . . . . . . . . . . . . . . . . . . . . . . . . . . .

## Background

Backtrack here to circa AD 65, approximately the same time
Paul wrote 1 Timothy. This letter covers many of the same subjects, but Paul addressed this letter to the missionary Titus, who
worked through similar issues with congregations on the island
of Crete.

## Summary

Cretans were a famously rough crowd, and there were those in
the church who sowed division and promoted false teachings.

Paul wrote to encourage his companion and convert, Titus, who had been his helper on his missionary journeys and traveled with him often. Paul encouraged Titus to teach the Cretans to lead exemplary lives, centered on the truth and on good works, so as to silence their critics and drown out lies with truth and goodness.

## Reflections

1. How can a life well lived, full of goodness and truth, actively fight deception and evil in the world? How can you commit to fight against evil with good?

_____

_____

_____

2. What similarities do you see between this book and 1 Timothy? What differences?

_____

_____

_____

3. What do you learn about good leadership in this book?

_____

_____

_____

4. How does God's grace "train" us? How has it trained you?

_____

_____

_____

# Philemon

*If then you count me as a partner, receive him as you would me. But if he has wronged you or owes anything, put that on my account.*

PHILEMON VV. 17–18

. . . . . . . . . . . . . . . . . . . . . . . . . . . . . .

## READING PLAN
½ day; 1 chapter a day; read with Titus

## THEMES
forgiveness and reconciliation; brotherhood under Christ

## MAJOR PLAYERS
Onesimus, Paul, Philemon

. . . . . . . . . . . . . . . . . . . . . . . . . . . . . .

## Background

Backtracking yet again, we see Paul in Rome, circa AD 62, writing either from prison or from his own home under house arrest (around the same time as when he wrote Colossians). Paul wrote to his friend Philemon, a good church leader in Colossae whom Paul had led to Christ years prior.

## Summary

Paul wrote to Philemon on behalf of Onesimus, a slave who had stolen money from Philemon and escaped to Rome. Onesimus gave his life to Christ, and he became one of Paul's most treasured friends and collaborators for the gospel. Eventually, both Onesimus and Paul decided it was time to seek forgiveness from Philemon. The penalty for stealing in Rome was death, but Paul wrote with grace, tact, and courtesy to ask Philemon to forgive his friend and to charge Onesimus's wrongdoing "to his account." Many draw a connection between Paul taking on responsibility for Onesimus and Jesus taking on our own sins.

## Reflections

1. Martin Luther said, "We are all [the Lord's] Onesimi." What does this mean? How did Jesus charge all your wrongdoings to His account?

_____

_____

2. What were some of the hurdles to reconciliation that Onesimus and Philemon faced? Culturally? Personally? What are some hurdles to reconciliation you've faced with people who have done you wrong?

_____

_____

3. What does it mean to pursue reconciliation "for love's sake" (v. 9), as Paul described?

_____

_____

_____

4. What stands out to you most in your reading of Philemon?

_____

_____

# Hebrews

Therefore we also, since we are surrounded by so great
a cloud of witnesses, let us lay aside every weight, and
the sin which so easily ensnares us, and let us run
with endurance the race that is set before us, looking
unto Jesus, the author and finisher of our faith.

HEBREWS 12:1–2

. . . . . . . . . . . . . . . . . . . . . . . . . . . . . .

## READING PLAN
3 days; 4 chapters a day

## THEMES
new covenant; Jesus is supreme; endurance, commitment,
and faith

## MAJOR PLAYERS
Jewish believers, Melchizedek, Old Testament heroes

. . . . . . . . . . . . . . . . . . . . . . . . . . . . . .

## Background

We don't know for sure who wrote the letter to the Hebrews or
to the Jewish Christians in Palestine. Some say Paul; some say
Luke, Barnabas, Silas, Philip, or Aquila and Priscilla. Whoever
it was, Hebrews was written during the AD 60s, before the
destruction of the temple in Jerusalem.

## Summary

The Jewish Christians gave up a lot to follow Christ—their religious and cultural heritage and, sometimes, their families as they were excommunicated. The writer here emphasized that Christ is the culmination of that tradition, above all others, and the Gift that came to the world through the Jewish nation. Temple rites, animal sacrifices, and the Levitical priesthood weren't necessary anymore; Christ fulfilled everything in a new covenant, better than the old. For those who were in danger of falling away, the writer encouraged them to endure, just as we also are encouraged.

## Reflections

1. Look for the phrases "once for all" and "eternal" in this letter. What did Jesus accomplish one time that superseded the rites that the Hebrews were concerned about?

   _____

   _____

   _____

   _____

2. What is the difference between the old covenant and the new covenant? How can we put our complete trust in this new covenant even today?

   _____

   _____

   _____

   _____

3. At what points have you found it difficult to endure in your faith? At what points have you come closest to falling away? How does the encouragement in Hebrews speak to you? How does Hebrews give you the strength and encouragement that you have everything you need to strengthen your faith and that God supplies all you need?

_____

_____

_____

_____

_____

_____

4. The writer of Hebrews reminded believers that the blessings of Jesus were better than anything else out there. What kinds of things tend to do for us what religious tradition did for the Hebrews—that is, distract us today from the freedom we have in Christ? Traditions? Wealth? Old ties to people? Family? Cultural systems? Career pursuits?

_____

_____

_____

_____

_____

_____

_____

# James

*If any of you lacks wisdom, let him ask of God, who gives to all liberally and without reproach, and it will be given to him.*

JAMES 1:5

. . . . . . . . . . . . . . . . . . . . . . . . . . . . .

## READING PLAN
1 day; 5 chapters a day

## THEMES
wisdom for Christian life; the tongue; prayer

## MAJOR PLAYERS
James, Jewish Christians

. . . . . . . . . . . . . . . . . . . . . . . . . . . . .

## Background

While we're not exactly sure which James wrote this book, many conclude that it was James the brother of Jesus, a devout Jewish convert who initially didn't believe in Jesus' divinity but was convinced and became a leader in the spread of the Christian faith. He was martyred by stoning circa AD 62, so this book was written earlier—possibly as early as the AD 40s.

## Summary

James addressed a lot of practical issues in this book that are still helpful to us today. We can find a lot of wisdom here, especially in matters of the tongue, the power of our speech, money, the rich, faith and works, and perseverance. He covered sticky topics such as unanswered prayers and worldliness and left us with a treasury of solid guidance.

## Reflections

1. What is your experience with the balance between faith and works? In which area can you grow?

_____

_____

_____

_____

_____

_____

2. Have you ever experienced trouble as a result of your words? Or felt the results of the positive power of your words? Describe those times and how the advice of James applies.

_____

_____

_____

_____

_____

_____

_____

_____

3. James appealed to the "brethren" a lot, which indicates that these were community instructions as well as individual instructions. What in James stands out to you as something you'd like to see more of in your community? What does your community excel at?

_____

_____

_____

_____

_____

_____

_____

_____

4. How is your search for wisdom going? What did James say about this search?

_____

_____

_____

_____

_____

_____

_____

_____

_____

# 1 Peter

In this you greatly rejoice, though now for a little while,
if need be, you have been grieved by various trials.

· · · · · · · · · · · · · · · · · · · · · · · · · · · · · ·

## READING PLAN
1 day; 5 chapters a day

## THEMES
encouragement through suffering; hope of heaven

## MAJOR PLAYERS
churches of Asia Minor, Mark, Peter

· · · · · · · · · · · · · · · · · · · · · · · · · · · · · ·

## Background

Peter, the leader of the twelve apostles, wrote near the end of
his life to encourage churches in modern-day Turkey, or Asia
Minor. This would have been near the time of the persecution
of Christians under the emperor Nero, which raged from AD
64 to AD 67. Suffering was certain, but Peter wrote to encourage them.

## Summary

Christians were being killed for sport in the Roman Empire, and
persecution was on the minds of those in Peter's audience. Paul

may have been recently executed, so it's possible that Peter wrote this letter to the churches Paul had founded to give them hope and tell them to keep the faith. While they were to prepare for suffering, they could do so with hope and rejoicing and with love toward one another.

## Reflections

1. How are suffering and glory connected in Christ? How do Christians become closer to Christ in suffering? Do you have any experience with this?

_____

_____

_____

_____

_____

_____

_____

2. How does keeping your eyes on eternity—on the big picture—help in times of suffering?

_____

_____

_____

_____

_____

_____

_____

3. Do you think of heaven as your home? Why or why not?

_____

_____

_____

_____

_____

_____

_____

_____

_____

_____

4. Look for the word *precious* and the concept of preciousness in this letter. What things show themselves to be of true value in trying times?

_____

_____

_____

_____

_____

_____

_____

_____

_____

_____

# 2 Peter

His divine power has given to us all things that pertain to life and godliness,
through the knowledge of Him who called us by glory and virtue.

2 PETER 1:3

. . . . . . . . . . . . . . . . . . . . . . . . . . . . . . .

READING PLAN
1 day; 3 chapters a day

THEMES
fruitfulness; warnings of false teachers

MAJOR PLAYERS
churches of Asia Minor, Peter

. . . . . . . . . . . . . . . . . . . . . . . . . . . . .

## Background

This second letter is thought to have been written shortly before
Peter's death (which, as tradition tells us, was an upside-down
crucifixion under the persecutions of Nero) or by an inspired
person writing in his voice shortly after his death circa AD 67.

## Summary

This short letter reinforces the truth of Peter's accounts, the
importance of staying the course, and how critical it is to hold
to true teachings and reject deception and false teachers. In the
rising tension of these days, some wondered when or whether

Jesus would come again; Peter assured them that the timing was not as important as the fact of His coming. God keeps His promises.

## Reflections

1. Why was this book's subject matter so important to remember? What would you choose as the most important topics to write about if you knew the end was coming?

_____

_____

2. Have you ever felt frustration or fear in the face of time's passing? What helps you focus less on the anxiety often associated with time's passing and more on being present and enjoying every moment with a thankful heart?

_____

_____

3. Have you had an experience with false teachers or teachings? How did you know? What can you learn from Peter about guarding against these things?

_____

_____

4. In the cycle of fruitfulness described in chapter 1, how do all these things "added to" each other build on and produce positive change? How can you commit to growth in each area described by verses 5–8?

_____

_____

_____

# 1 John

Beloved, if God so loved us, we also ought to love one another.

1 JOHN 4:11

. . . . . . . . . . . . . . . . . . . . . . . . . . . . . . . . . . . .

## READING PLAN
1 day; 5 chapters a day

## THEMES
Jesus' reality; what Christians are like; the importance of love

## MAJOR PLAYERS
churches around Ephesus, John

. . . . . . . . . . . . . . . . . . . . . . . . . . . . . . . .

## Background

Here at the end of the Bible, we have three short books by John, and the first was likely meant to be a circular letter to congregations in and around Ephesus. These are the latest writings in the New Testament, circa AD 85–95.

## Summary

The book of 1 John does a good job of answering the question: "What makes a Christian?" This was important because there were so many competing teachings circulating within the church introduced by the Gnostics, who were people convinced they had special knowledge over and above what the apostles taught (*gnosis*

= "knowledge"). John combatted their teachings by reconfirming what he knew firsthand about Jesus: He walked as a real man, and He is really the risen Son of God. John also emphasized love as a characteristic of those who have truly been transformed by Christ.

## Reflections

1. Keep track of what John said "we know" about Jesus, God, and our faith. How did this combat shaky teachings of the day, and how does it do the same today?

   _____

   _____

2. If Gnostics were so focused on their special, secret "knowledge," how did John make a case for the completeness of the gospel as it had been taught?

   _____

   _____

3. Make note of stark contrasts in this letter (darkness and light, righteousness and sin, etc.). How do we know the difference between one or the other?

   _____

   _____

   _____

4. How do we know and feel what real love is? How did John offer us help to strengthen our understanding? What does it mean for you on a daily basis to "walk in the light" (1:7)?

   _____

   _____

   _____

# 2 John

Love one another.

2 John v. 5

. . . . . . . . . . . . . . . . . . . . . . . . . . . . . .

## READING PLAN
1/3 day; 1 chapter a day; read with 3 John and Jude

## THEMES
love; obedience; warning against deceivers

## MAJOR PLAYERS
elect lady, John (the Elder)

. . . . . . . . . . . . . . . . . . . . . . . . . . . .

## Background

This is one of John's rare personal letters, not necessarily meant for circulation but useful, nonetheless. The elect lady he spoke of was likely a church leader.

## Summary

This quick note was sent to an unknown lady of the church to encourage her to hold fast to the truth in the face of intruders who introduced untruths into the community. Some wolves in sheep's clothing apparently had taken advantage of their hospitality and brought in dangerous teachings. John advised her to have nothing to do with them and to prioritize love.

# Reflections

1. How are God's love and commandments interlaced?

_____

_____

_____

_____

_____

_____

_____

_____

_____

2. Can love exist without truth? How should we look out for
   untruth in our lives?

_____

_____

_____

_____

_____

_____

_____

_____

_____

# 3 John

*I have no greater joy than to hear that my children walk in truth.*

3 JOHN V. 4

. . . . . . . . . . . . . . . . . . . . . . . . . . . . . . . . . .

## READING PLAN
1/3 day; 1 chapter a day; read with 2 John and Jude

## THEMES
hospitality; love and truth; church life

## MAJOR PLAYERS
Demetrius, Diotrephes, Gaius, John

. . . . . . . . . . . . . . . . . . . . . . . . . . . . . . . . . .

## Background

John, the "Elder" mentioned in the opening line, wrote from Ephesus near the end of his ministry circa AD 85–90. He wrote to one of the smaller churches, perhaps in Asia, that Paul originally started. This is the second personal letter we have from John (in addition to 2 John). This is also the shortest book in the Bible.

## Summary

In this early church slice of life, we see John's personal words to his friend and protégé, Gaius, and also a faithful friend and leader of a church. John praised Gaius for being welcoming to a group of itinerant preachers doing God's work and for providing hospitality, material support, and a good example to all churches. In contrast, we have Diotrephes, an egoistic leader of another church likely in the same city. Diotrephes had rejected those preachers before Gaius took them in.

## Reflections

1. What value did John assign to hospitality? How can you devote yourself more to hospitality in your everyday life?

_____

_____

_____

_____

_____

_____

_____

2. How many times did John mention truth? What is the importance of walking in truth, working for truth, and witnessing truthfully? How about, especially for the early church, where people like Diotrephes caused trouble?

_____

_____

_____

_____

_____

_____

# Jude

Contend earnestly for the faith which was
once for all delivered to the saints.

Jude v. 3

. . . . . . . . . . . . . . . . . . . . . . . . . . . . .

## READING PLAN
1/3 day; 1 chapter a day; read with 2 John and 3 John

## THEMES
warning about apostates

## MAJOR PLAYERS
Enoch (son of Cain), Jude, Michael (angel)

. . . . . . . . . . . . . . . . . . . . . . . . . . . . .

## Background

There are several Judes in the Bible (a.k.a. Judah and Judas), but
most scholars agree that this book is from Jude, the brother of
Jesus, likely written in a hurry circa AD 67 to warn a church of
bad actors in its midst.

## Summary

The content of Jude may remind you of 2 Peter, which forewarned
about false teachers. At the point of this writing, those dangerous
people had arrived and had intentionally tried to undermine the
church. This has continued to be a problem throughout church

history. Jude also referred to some sources we no longer have, all to illustrate the differences between godliness and ungodliness—and to harshly condemn those who would try to pull the church apart.

## Reflections

1. Jude let loose on the apostates with some very harsh language. What do Jude and other New Testament writers say about how to deal with intentionally destructive people? How can you still uphold the light inside of you when facing such people?

_____

_____

_____

_____

_____

_____

2. How do you protect yourself from untruth? How can you help those around you? How have others helped to keep you lifted and protected you against untruth?

_____

_____

_____

_____

_____

_____

# Revelation

"I am the Alpha and the Omega, the Beginning
and the End," says the Lord, "who is and who
was and who is to come, the Almighty."

REVELATION 1:8

. . . . . . . . . . . . . . . . . . . . . . . . . . . . . .

## READING PLAN
6 days; 4 chapters a day

## THEMES
final victory of Jesus; description of the new heavens and new
earth; things to come

## MAJOR PLAYERS
cast of descriptive and symbolic characters, Jesus, John, Satan,
the seven churches

. . . . . . . . . . . . . . . . . . . . . . . . . . . . . .

## Background

While the apostle John was exiled on the island of Patmos during
a period of persecution, he received a sweeping vision from Jesus
about the end of the world as we know it and the coming of a
new world. It was likely written circa AD 95, during the reign of
the emperor Domitian.

# Summary

This grand and complex book, the ultimate ending to our story and the story of God's people told in the Bible, is to be read with an open mind, an open heart, and great humility. Have some study resources at hand as you go, and remember that only God knows for sure what many of John's visions really mean. But what *we* know for sure is that Jesus is victorious, He will reign in heaven and on earth, and the human story has a hopeful end because of the salvation He offers. This revelation or "apocalyptic" account may have some familiar imagery, as you look back over similar accounts in Ezekiel, Daniel, and Zechariah. This time, though, you see the culmination of history in light of Christ.

When John wrote, the Christians were besieged by threats and fears similar to that of the children of Israel returning from Babylonian exile in the Old Testament. They had been worn down by systematic persecution and were in need of a vision from God to give them a way to chart the future. But the Israelites were not wiped out—the church still remained—and today, thousands of years later, we are the result. While many mysteries await us in times ahead and the story between God and His people on earth is not over, we can know that its ending will be glorious—and that Jesus is our Hope.

# *Reflections*

1. How does John describe Christ, the Lamb, in Revelation? How do these descriptions and the ones you've encountered on your journey through the Bible informed the way you see Him now?

_____

_____

_____

_____

_____

_____

_____

_____

2. How has your understanding of God's eternity and intentions toward His people grown as you've gone from Genesis to Revelation?

_____

_____

_____

_____

_____

_____

_____

_____

_____

3. Having read the Bible from start to finish, and in light of
   John's prophecies, what do you now know for sure? What do
   you want to continue to learn more about? What aspects would
   you like to strengthen your knowledge about?

   _____

   _____

   _____

   _____

   _____

   _____

   _____

   _____

   _____


4. Now that you know the beginning and end of humankind's
   story, how will that change how you live out your part of the
   middle—your own testament, your own story? How have the
   events and discoveries of the past year been a part of that story?

   _____

   _____

   _____

   _____

   _____

   _____

   _____

   _____

   _____

5. What were the highs and lows of this journey through the Bible for you? Reflect on how far you came, and celebrate. In what new ways will you continue to seek God and His truth in the coming year?

_____

_____

_____

_____

_____

_____

_____

_____

_____

_____

_____

_____

_____

_____

_____

_____

_____

_____

_____

_____